THREE CHOIRS FESTIVAL
in ten concerts

THREE CHOIRS FESTIVAL
in ten concerts

Simon Carpenter

LOGASTON PRESS

FRONTISPIECE: Roy Massey with the Festival chorus in Hereford Cathedral in 1991 (© Gareth Rees-Roberts). FRONT COVER, TOP ROW, LEFT TO RIGHT: Ralph Vaughan Williams at the 1954 Worcester Festival (© Brendan Kerney, with kind permission of the Kerney Family Creative Collection); Maria Caradori-Allan, lithograph by Henri Grevedon, 1831 (public domain); Gloucester Cathedral during the 1922 Festival (© The British Library Board. All rights reserved. With thanks to The British Newspaper Archive). MIDDLE ROW, LEFT TO RIGHT: George Frideric Handel, painting attributed to Balthasar Denner (public domain); Hereford Cathedral, 1837 (courtesy of Derek Foxton). BOTTOM IMAGE: Roy Massey with the Festival Chorus in Hereford Cathedral in 1991 (© Gareth Rees-Roberts)

First published 2024 by Logaston Press
The Holme, Church Road, Eardisley HR3 6NJ
www.logastonpress.co.uk
An imprint of Fircone Books Ltd.

ISBN 978-1-910839-75-1

Designed and typeset by Richard Wheeler in 11 on 15 Garamond.
Cover design by Richard Wheeler.

Printed and bound in the Czech Republic.

Logaston Press is committed to a sustainable future for our business, our readers and our planet. The book in your hands is made from paper certified by the Forest Stewardship Council.

British Library Catalogue in Publishing Data.
A CIP catalogue record for this book is available from the British Library.

contents

foreword   VII

acknowledgements   IX

preface   XI

1   Handel's *Messiah*: Gloucester, 1757   1

2   The move to the nave: Hereford, 1834   13

3   Hubert Parry: Gloucester, 1868   25

4   Female composers: Hereford, 1882   41

5   Edward Elgar: Worcester, 1890   53

6   Ralph Vaughan Williams: Gloucester, 1910   71

7   Herbert Howells: Gloucester, 1922   85

8   Gustav Holst: Gloucester, 1925   97

9   Gerald Finzi: Hereford, 1949   113

10   Applause at last: Worcester, 1969   125

key figures mentioned in the text   137

bibliography   153

index   155

The aim of music is the glory of God and pleasant recreation.
Attributed to J.S. Bach, as quoted by Gustav Holst

foreword

How do we begin to understand musical history? Many books have been devoted to 'great' composers and their music, but arguably it's all meaningless without their context. What music was played, and why, and by whom? For so many of the composers in this book, it was a sense of the places and friendships above all that drove their musical endeavours. Music comes to represent people, places, and relationships. Breaking it down – *three* choirs, *three* cathedrals, *ten* concerts – *seems* a very logical way to get your head around it. However, what emerges is a wonderfully human sense of the messiness of history, the interconnectedness of everything, and how some things never change.

At the 2023 Gloucester Festival, I spoke about Ralph Vaughan Williams' *Fantasia on a Theme by Thomas Tallis* (see Chapter 6), a piece that seems to confront my opening question head-on. It's a piece about *hearing* history. I stood in the empty nave of Gloucester and tried to imagine what it was like to hear it for the first time. But what struck me most was how little the view had changed. The Norman architecture gives an incredible sense of timelessness, as if Tallis or Vaughan Williams (or both) might walk around the corner from the transept at any point! The piece plays with that sense of historical confusion: we have elements which seem to echo the earliest chant through to the most 'modern' string sonorities of Ravel, all based on a sixteenth-century tune. To add to the confusion, the whole thing is a form of *concerto grosso* – a Baroque form resurrected in Elgar's celebrated *Introduction and Allegro*, but with all the parallel lines of Debussy's latest scores. And is that magical opening a paraphrase of the opening of Elgar's *The Apostles* (a mysticism he found in Wagner's *Ring*)? It's an incredible synthesis of musical elements, which led one critic to ask: am I listening to something 'very old or very new?'

For me, what emerges from this book is a sense of how the Festival *itself* has always inhabited a similar position, mediating the 'very old or very new'. History and tradition have always mattered to its identity, but the Festival continues to champion new music, establishing new relationships between cathedral musicians and the wonderful array of incoming talent. In that sense, the narratives of British music history continue – the choral tradition, the history of the oratorio genre, and the continuing evolution of pastoralism.

There's also a strong sense of the challenges faced and attitudes transformed: from the ongoing tensions between the sacred and the secular, the professionalisation of the organisation and funding, and the embracing of social and cultural change. The book, like all good writing, raises as many questions as it answers. Attitudes towards concerts in cathedral naves, female composers, applause and even the direction that seats face, give a fascinating insight into how relatively recently aspects of our cultural lives have changed. Likewise, Simon frequently draws upon elements of critical reception that might surprise us now. The 'Tallis' *Fantasia*, for example, was not the overwhelming success that its current popularity might suggest, and this demonstrates the risk that the Festival continues to take to remain so culturally relevant and vital: bringing together amateurs and professionals, the sacred and secular, the large and the small, listeners from home and abroad, and performers from across the globe. All with a sense of pilgrimage and of ritual that has become part of it – a living history.

Jonathan Clinch
Royal Academy of Music
March 2024

acknowledgements

This book is dedicated to, and the fruit of the encouragement and support of, many people, among them being:

Firstly my family: my wife Anita and my children, James and Anne, and my daughter-in-law, Jess.

And then to Anthony Boden, author of what is still the main reference source for the history of the Festival.

Naomi Belshaw, the chair of the Three Choirs Festival, Alexis Paterson, chief executive, and all the Festival staff past and present since I started volunteering in 2020: Isabella Abbot Parker, Bryony Boyes-Hannis, Roger Collcott, Robert Convey, Anna Crosby, Helen Gatenby, Rachael Hall, Nicola Lawson, Catherine Lewen, Lucy Potter, Jessica Robson-Hill, Hannah Roper, September Turner and Joseph Wong.

The present directors of music at the three cathedrals: Adrian Partington (Gloucester), Geraint Bowen (Hereford) and Samuel Hudson (Worcester).

Gloucester Choral Society, and all my friends in it.

My old University of Gloucestershire tutors, Christian O'Connell and Melanie Ilic – for helping me believe that I am a historian.

All three Three Choirs cathedral librarians: Rebecca Phillips (Gloucester), David Morrison (Worcester) and Elizabeth Semper O'Keefe (Hereford).

The members of the Three Choirs Festival Research Group.

All who have helped with general encouragement, research, preparing the text and illustrations, notably: Richard Auckland, Alice Bingham, Richard Bratby, Kerensa Briggs, Alexandra Coghlan, Jeremy Dibble, Richard Dixon, Robert Flute, Derek Foxton, Robert Garbolinski, Marcus Green, Ally Hardy, Clare Horacek, Peter Horton, Aeden Kerney, Laura Kinnear, Philip Lancaster, Candia McKormack, Philip Lancaster, John Miller, Andrew

Millinger, John Rowlands, Paul Spicer, Clare Stevens, Paul Sumsion, Sarah Todd, Philippa Tudor and Clare Wichbold.

I am grateful to so many other people for their help and support, not just with this book, but with the day-to-day work I do as volunteer with the Festival. I particularly want to pick out Dr Jonathan Clinch for his unwavering helpfulness and encouragement since my early days of volunteering, and for writing the foreword. I also want to thank here the various copyright holders for the use of their material.

One person not named there, but who is responsible as much as anyone for this book, is Dr Barry Rose, my Guildford choirmaster. It was the standards he set, and the self-discipline, time management and teamwork skills that he installed in all of us that shaped me as the person I am now, and who along the way introduced me to the music of S.S. Wesley, Parry, Elgar, Vaughan Williams, Howells, Sumsion, Brewer et al.

Thank you all so much.

preface

For the last few years I have had the privilege to be the volunteer archivist and historian for the Three Choirs Festival. As an ex-cathedral chorister (Guildford), steeped in the Anglican choral tradition, and the possessor of a recent postgraduate degree in history (for which I researched the teaching career of former Gloucester Cathedral organist, Sir Herbert Brewer), it was and is my dream job.

In the early months of my time in post, my 'bibles' as I read around, and researched the history of the Festival in order to bring myself up to speed with it were the official *Annals*, the Watkins Shaw and the Boden histories of the Festival. These are invaluable for any serious student of the Festival's history and I constantly refer back to them.

A feature of the Festival over its long history is its championing of new music. Soon after joining the team, the idea of producing a book around the premiere debuts of some of the composers most associated with it took shape in my mind. Eight names immediately sprang to mind, now constituting the middle chapters of this book. I then tried out the idea on Alexis Paterson and Tony Boden just before Christmas 2021. They liked it as well, and were most encouraging; in fact, what is now Chapter 10 was Alexis' suggestion. To cover the early years, I turned to a work long-associated with the Festival: Handel's *Messiah*. I then approached Logaston Press, as the three counties' leading local history publisher, with the result you are now holding. My hope for my contribution to the Festival's recorded history is that it complements the comprehensive approach of my predecessors' work by providing an accessible overview of the Festival's history over its 300-plus years. I am also pleased that it highlights some of the leading female composers who have featured over the years.

Handel's *Messiah*

Boothall, Gloucester: 16 September 1757

On Friday 16 September 1757 the audience in the Boothall Gloucester was treated to the Three Choirs Festival and the city's first performance of Handel's Messiah, *a work that had been enthusiastically received everywhere since being premiered in Dublin 15 years earlier in 1742.*

IT WAS ALMOST certainly included on the programme due to the initiative of that year's Festival director, William Hayes, the former Worcester Cathedral organist and, by then, Professor of Music at Oxford University. He was a major champion of Handel and one of the most active conductors of his oratorios outside London. Among the orchestra and soloists were some of the top names of that age, and the chorus comprised the choirs of the three cathedrals plus other members of the three cities' music clubs.

Messiah: the birth of a musical icon

Messiah is an oratorio (a large-scale musical work for orchestra and voices typically on a sacred theme) to a libretto selected from the King James Bible and the Coverdale Psalter by Handel's friend, Charles Jennens. It was composed in a few weeks between August and September 1741, although Handel did adapt parts of it from others of his works. Its first performance was in Dublin in April 1742, and its first London performance was in 1743. There is no single definitive version available, and the full score wasn't published until 1767. In the meantime, the piece appeared in dribs and drabs. The Overture was published in 1743, and arias were included in volumes of

George Frideric Handel (1685–1759), composer of the oratorio *Messiah*. Painting attributed to Balthasar Denner, 1726–28 (© National Portrait Gallery, London)

Handel's *Songs selected from the oratorios.* Around 20 of the work's movements were available by Handel's death in 1759, but not the complete work.

However, performances had started taking place around the country by 1749 when it opened the Radcliffe Camera in Oxford, and these performances in the provinces, including that at the Three Choirs Festival, represented forms of the work uninfluenced by changes made by Handel after 1745. Hayes would have been responsible for pulling the work together for the Three Choirs Festival and was known to not being above 'improving' Handel where he felt it was necessary.

The 'gloomy and overcrowded' concert venue – the Boothall, Westgate Street, Gloucester. Originally built in 1192, it was rebuilt in 1607 and demolished in 1957

Following its Three Choirs appearance in secular venues in 1757 and 1758, the performance at the 1759 Festival was in Hereford Cathedral. *Messiah* began by being programmed in neutral venues because at that time oratorio was considered 'secular' and it was considered improper for non-liturgical music to take place in a consecrated building.

The concert hall: gloomy and overcrowded

Gloucester's Boothall, until it was demolished in 1957, was on the south side of Westgate Street adjoining Shire Hall. Originally built in 1192, by the time of the *Messiah* concert it was in the guise of its 1607 rebuild, which included a great hall occupying the full height of the building, its roof supported by a double row of chestnut pillars. It was used as an entertainment venue by this time; however, as a concert hall it was by no means ideal as it was gloomy and tended to become overcrowded and heated. Despite these inconveniences, it was used as such by the Festival from at least 1748 until 1817 when the secular concerts moved next door to Shire Hall. It was the original seat of government of the town as well as playing an important role in its commercial life. From at least the early fourteenth century there was also an inn on the site which fronted the street.

The performers

In contrast to later ages, which tried to cram as many items into a concert as possible, *Messiah* was the only item on the programme that Friday, the first time that performances at Gloucester Festivals had been extended to a third evening. The assembled audience would have seen in front of them a choir of maybe 50 voices. The orchestra, as listed in the local media, was made up of three trumpets, a pair of kettle drums, four hautboys, four bassoons, two double basses, violins and violoncelloes. And the soloists were among the leading names of the time including Giulia Frasi and John Beard. At this time the soloists were the main draw for audiences, as they would be for some time to come. The conductor was William Hayes. As was the custom, there was a ball following the concert in the same venue, where there would have been more music, food and dancing.

William Hayes

At this time, it wasn't the custom for the local cathedral organist to direct the Festival concerts, and William Hayes also directed the next two Gloucester Festivals, in 1760 and 1763. A leading composer, organist, singer and academic, he was born in Gloucester and was a chorister of his home cathedral between 1717 and 1727, moving up to becoming assistant organist. He went on to be appointed Organist of Shrewsbury in 1729, Worcester Cathedral in 1731 and Magdalen College, Oxford in 1734, where he gained a BMus in 1735 and DMus in 1749. In 1741 he was elected Heather Professor of Music and organist of the university church. He presided over Oxford concert life for 30 years and was instrumental in the building of the Holywell Music Room in 1748, the oldest purpose-built concert hall in Europe. An enthusiastic Handelian, and one of the most active conductors of his oratorios and other large-scale works outside London, he had conducted *Messiah* at Bath and Bristol in 1755 and 1756. In addition, he was deputy steward for the 1754 Festival.

William Hayes (1706–77)
(© National Portrait Gallery, London)

To see and be seen

In the eighteenth and early nineteenth centuries, Three Choirs Festival audiences were the local gentry, clergy and other professionals and the well-to-do. In general, for the aristocracy, social appearance at an event was of more significance than the music, and the Festivals at each centre exercised a growing attraction for, as the local papers described them, 'persons of quality and distinction' and the 'nobility and gentry' in the three shires and beyond. The 1726 meeting at Worcester, according to the *Worcester Weekly Journal*, successfully attracted 'an handsome appearance of gentry'. The same people also patronised festivals at Bath, Brighton and in London. Many would not only have attended the concerts but also the local races scheduled for the same time and the balls which usually followed the evening concerts, using the same halls as was the case on this occasion. According to the *Annals* (the official history of the Festival, first published in 1812), in its report of the Festival, Handel's 'sublime and popular oratorio' of the *Messiah* 'was received at Gloucester with rapturous applause'. Presumably the author, Daniel Lysons (1762–1834), must have received that feedback from someone who was there since it happened a few years before he was born.

The rest of the Festival

The festival began for the performers on Monday 12 September when they were, according to the *Oxford Journal*, 'expected to be at Gloucester ... early enough to rehearse one of the pieces intended for the evening's performance', which left the time open to some interpretation.

For the audience, the Gloucester races (held at a course on Sud Meadow since the 1720s), was the main social event of the season for the county gentry and had drawn them into the city each year. Every third year from 1736, it coincided with the Music Meeting, but since the 1740s it had only been held in the years the Music Meeting was in the city. In 1757 the main race was held the day before the Music Meeting started. In 1757 both events also shared a steward, Norborne Berkeley, of whom more later.

On Tuesday 13 September a plate of 50 pounds was run, according to the *Oxford Journal*, for 'any horse, mare or gelding of four years old carrying nine stone who never won a Royal Plate; five year olds to carry nine stone; six year olds ten stone; and Aged ten stone and seven pounds'. This was followed by ordinaries (refreshments provided by the steward) at the White Swan inn, upper Northgate Street. The music stewards' dinner was held in the Bell, Southgate Street, that evening, followed by a ball.

The Festival opened on Wednesday 14 September with a service in the cathedral. This included Purcell's *Te Deum* and two of Handel's Coronation Anthems. That evening in the Boothall, Handel's *Judas Maccabeus* was performed, followed by a ball in the same location and ordinaries in the Bell.

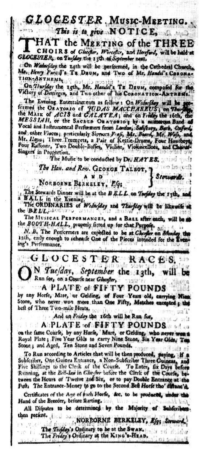

Advertisements for the forthcoming
Gloucester Music Meeting and Gloucester
Races in the *Oxford Journal*, 3 September
1757 (© The British Library Board)

On the following day the cathedral service included Handel's *Dettingen Te Deum* and two other Coronation Anthems by the same composer. In the afternoon Handel's *Acis and Galatea* (a work that has been variously described as a serenata, a masque, a pastoral or pastoral opera, a 'little opera', an entertainment and an oratorio) was performed in the Boothall, followed by a ball and ordinaries in the Bell. And then on Friday afternoon was *Messiah*. This was followed by a ball in the Boothall and race ordinaries in the King's Head, Westgate Street.

At this time, the Bell, White Swan and King's Head were three of the leading inns in the city, and regularly hosted corporation and other prestigious dinners.

The main men: the stewards

For this Festival, the Hon. and Revd George Talbot and Norborne Berkeley were the stewards, and Norborne Berkeley was also the steward of the race meeting. This meant that not only were they the sole executive officers, with full responsibility for promoting, organising and advertising the meetings, but they had the additional burden of whatever financial deficit there might be. From the inception of the Festival and up to 1754 there had only been one steward, a member of one of the choirs. But from 1755 this was altered at all three centres to two stewards, one clerical and one lay, both to be of considerable standing in the diocese. This marks the beginning of a long association of the leading county families with this office

Steward of the 1757 Festival, the Right Honourable Norborne Berkeley (c.1717–70) (Courtesy of the New York Public Library)

and also of the bishops and deans. For both stewards, this was the only occasion they undertook this role, although Norborne Berkeley is listed as having acted as the charity steward for the 1744 (Hereford) Festival.

At this time, Norborne Berkeley (1717–70) was a member of the House of Commons as a knight of the shire for Gloucestershire, a seat he held until 1763. A member of the Stoke Gifford branch of the Berkeley family, he later, as Baron Botetourt, was Royal Governor of the colony of Virginia from 1768 until his death in 1770. Earlier, he had aided the early spa developments in Cheltenham, collaborating with Henry Skillicorne in the development of the well walks in the Bayshill area of the town in 1739–40.

A few years after this Festival, the Hon. and Revd George Talbot (the third son of the leading lawyer and politician, Charles, first Baron Talbot) married the Honourable Anne Bouverie, the daughter of Jacob, the 1st Viscount Folkestone, in 1761. He had grown up in his family's mansion in Glamorgan. Both were also principal benefactors of a 1754 scheme initially set up to provide a dispensary in Stroud and later also a county hospital in Gloucester.

£100 net profit

Hayes' fee for the Festival, including conducting and singing in *Judas Maccabeus*, *Acis and Galatea* and *Messiah*, was £27 6s, or half that of the leading soloist, Giulia Frasi. Included in this total was his fee for the considerable task of 'collecting, collating, writing and adjusting parts'. For these duties he received £5 5s.

In all, Hayes' accounts for the 1757 Festival show that there were 61 performing musicians in addition to the leading soloists Beard and Frasi, and Hayes himself. They were drawn from Bath, Salisbury, Worcester and Hereford as well as Gloucester. One of Hayes' sons, Thomas, sang as bass for the Festival for a fee of £10 10s. In all, their fees totalled £405 2s which was offset by the sale of tickets, which grossed £162 for *Judas Maccabeus*, £136 for *Acis and Galatea* and, even at first appearance, *Messiah* led with £207. This led to a net profit of £100.

The eighteenth-century Festival
It is not known what year the first Festival was held, but there is little doubt that it was around the years 1713–15. The earliest year for which firm documentary evidence exists is 1719, when it was reported in the Worcester press that members of the annual musical assembly were required to meet on 31 August for public performance on the following two days.

The Festival came into being through a desire on the part of the musical societies of Gloucester, Hereford and Worcester to participate in some form of cooperative music-making. It is known that the music societies in the three cities were largely run by the clergy of Gloucester, Hereford and Worcester prior to the establishment of the Festival itself. The original purpose was not therefore to raise money for charity, but this quickly became the assumed reason for the Festival's existence after regular formal collections had begun at the Gloucester Festival of 1724.

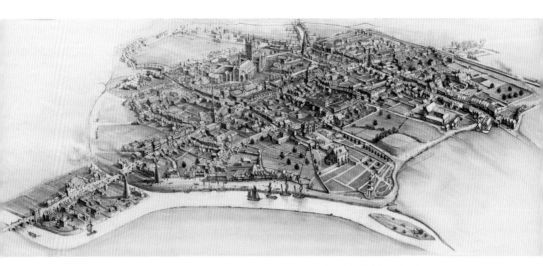

Gloucester as it may have looked in 1750 (© Philip Moss)

Much of the music performed in the early years centred around the works of Purcell, while his *Te Deum* and also that of William Croft are the first works of which we have any record. Professional musicians were first engaged from London in 1733. The earliest reference to Handel is at Gloucester in 1736 when his *Te Deum* was performed, while in 1738 Hereford gave his oratorio *Hester* and his *Alexander's Feast* was heard at Gloucester in 1739 'with Trumpets, French Horns and Kettle Drums'. In 1745 (Gloucester) the singers were joined by members of the choirs from the Chapel Royal, Westminster Abbey and St Paul's, all led by Maurice Greene 'Master of his Majesty's Band of Musick'.

The general schedule, as shown above, was already established by the middle of the century. Following a rehearsal on the Monday evening there was an opening service in the cathedral the next day, at which various anthems were performed with full orchestral accompaniment. An important part of this service was the sermon, which was usually based on some appropriate text concerning sacred music and charitable giving. The morning's events were followed by an evening concert which was at this stage devoted to the performance of an oratorio – usually a work by Handel – and the third day's schedule followed a similar pattern. In addition to this there would be a number of social events as indicated above, including balls, ordinaries and often a public breakfast on the final morning.

In Worcester, the secular concerts were first held in the Guildhall, but moved to College Hall in 1755 due to a dispute with the Corporation. From 1762, The Hereford secular concerts were held in the Music Room (part of the Cathedral School) which was enlarged in that year at the expense of local clergy on the understanding it would be used for that purpose.

Hereford added a third morning in 1759, and transferred *Messiah* to this time from the evening concert slot. This was the first departure from the previously-unbroken record of nothing but services and anthems within the cathedrals themselves.

Private hospitality during the Festivals grew in the second half of the century, in addition to the 'ordinaries' which provided lunch for the assembled company at the principal hostelries

The basis of the choral body was the combined cathedral choirs, but others were employed from the earliest times. Female chorus singers were engaged from 1772. Outstanding soloists were commissioned from the start. In the eighteenth century, vocalists were esteemed beyond all other virtuoso performers. Signora Galli (mezzo), William Savage and Gaetano Guadagni (counter tenor) regularly participated, and both the first and the last were amongst the most renowned singers of Handel's music – and, as they both had sang under composer himself, they had a special authority. The same is true of Giulia Frasi who sang in nine successive years from 1756, and John Beard, the notable tenor, who first established the popularity of that voice in England. As well as 1756, he appeared in 1755, 1757, 1758, 1759, 1760 and 1761.

The earliest reference to the make-up of the orchestra was for this 1757 Festival. Two French horns and tenor violas are mentioned in addition in 1760, and a pair of clarinets appear in 1763. Among the earliest big names, as well as Frasi and Beard mentioned above, were Felice de Giardini and Johann Christian Fischer. Giardini, who led the band for seven years from 1770, was one of the leading violinists in Europe.

The first conductors known to have directed the Festivals were not cathedral organists. These were William Boyce and, as outlined above, William Hayes. This is probably due to the fact that both men were successively conductor of the London-based Festival of the Sons of the Clergy. The first cathedral organist to be recorded as conductor was Richard Clack of Hereford, who oversaw the 1759 meeting. From 1788, the cathedral organist was habitually appointed by the stewards to conduct the meeting.

Messiah at the Festival

Messiah from the first was a special attraction. At the next Festival (1758) in Worcester, 1,000 people are said to have heard it on the third evening, as against 800 for Judas Maccabeus and 700 for Alexander's Feast by the same composer. And so, after a groundbreaking performance in Bristol Cathedral in 1758, the organisers of the Hereford Festival in 1759 decided to host a performance within their cathedral. With Worcester and Gloucester following suit in 1761 and 1769 respectively, it became customary from that time for all the oratorio performances, not just Messiah, to take place in the cathedrals. The evening concerts were then given over to more purely secular items such as short songs, popular operatic arias, glees, vocal ensembles and some instrumental pieces.

Performances of *Messiah* also quickly spread around the provinces. As was seen above, it reached Oxford in 1749, Salisbury in 1752 and, in 1755, Bath, directed by Hayes. In 1756, it was the work that the New Musick Room in Bristol was opened with. It was repeated in Bristol in 1757 and 1758. Of the latter performance, John Wesley (uncle of S.S. Wesley, later organist of Hereford and Gloucester) recorded in his journal:

> I went to the cathedral to hear Mr Handel's *Messiah*. I doubt if that congregation was ever so serious at a sermon as they were during this performance. In many places, especially in several of the choruses, it exceeded my expectations.

Messiah was also performed at the Three Choirs in whole or part every year, except for the 'mock' festival year of 1875, until the 1950s, and included in all but two Festivals to 1963. There was a special performance in 2001 on a Handel day, but otherwise it is now a very long way down the programming list, if anywhere.

2

The move to the nave

Hereford Cathedral: 10 September 1834

On Wednesday morning, 10 September 1834, to an accompaniment of heavy rain outside, an audience of over 730 witnessed almost the first ever Three Choirs Festival concert held in the nave of a cathedral. Up to that point they had been held in the choir area, apart from for a one-off visit from George III and the royal family in 1788 when the nave of Worcester cathedral was suitably fitted out for the occasion.

Why the move?

To MODERN MINDS this should probably read; why were they held in the choir for the first hundred years? The reason was that their official status was that of religious services. And, apart from the secular concerts, they began by being almost exclusively sung by the cathedral choirs, and the choir is the place in the cathedral where they performed. Practically, the move was to provide more space for the growing number of performers – as the orchestra grew, due to the development of musical style from baroque to classical, the chorus had to grow to keep the balance – and to be able to offer more accommodation for the audience. In 1823, the orchestra numbered 47 and the choir 130. There also wasn't enough space in the choir to employ the numbers of soloists that other festivals, such as Norwich and Birmingham, could. In 1810, only nine soloists were employed by the Three Choirs Festival, at a time when the star performer was still one of the big draws for audiences. In 1850, 16 years after the move, there were nearly 300 performers in total.

Performance of the *Messiah* in the nave of Hereford Cathedral,
Wednesday 27 September 1837 (courtesy of Derek Foxton)

A large assemblage of the rank and fashion

The move was also likely to have been at the prompting of the young new organist of Hereford, S.S. Wesley, on his way to becoming one of the leading musicians and composers of the nineteenth century. However, the official reason outlined in the *Annals* was to make the concerts more appealing to potential audience members:

> great exertions were used by the stewards to make it attractive. In their address to the public they say in furtherance of this view, as well as compliance with scruples to which they willingly defer, they have concurred with the Dean and Chapter in a determination to transfer the scene of the musical performance from the choir to the nave of the cathedral, where the more ample accommodation for the auditory, the impressive character of the architecture, and the improved sphere for the undulation of harmonious sounds, will combine to augment that unspeakable fascination which is the never-failing effect of the grand compositions selected for the occasion.

A few weeks after the Festival, the dean was quoted as saying that he, 'as an individual ... had done all in his power to render the meeting as little exclusive as possible, that all persons living around might participate in it.'

The ambition behind the 'great exertions' was outlined in the *Hereford Times* of 13 September:

> From the extensive preparations and activity which had for some time been manifest by the superintending powers, high hopes were entertained of a large assemblage of the rank and fashion of Herefordshire as well as the adjoining counties. These hopes we are gratified to add, were not disappointed; indeed we were confident that the Festival would pass off with éclat, for the corps of vocal and instrumental performers numbered many of the most celebrated of the day ... The orchestra complete, consisted of 120 performers of which 60 were instrumental and 60 vocal.

Creation and *The Last Judgement*

The 736 members of the audience were treated to a varied programme including Spohr's oratorio, *The Last Judgement*, the first part of Haydn's

Creation, an *Antiphona* by S. Wesley, the conductor's father and a *Sanctus* by S.S. Wesley himself. In addition, there were other selected pieces by Handel.

The view of the *Hereford Times*

The reporter from the *Hereford Times* was impressed. In his report he began by describing the effects of the move to the nave – first occurring on the previous day for the Festival's opening service – reassuring those that might be concerned by the development:

> The audience in the cathedral was upwards of 600, a larger number than were ever witnessed on the first day. As the performance was in the nave ... Let it be imagined that the nave had been for the occasion converted into a grand saloon; from the centre of the organ screen, or rather, its gallery, to within five or six feet from the floor, was the orchestra, occupying the full breadth between the pillars. The principal singers were ranged in the front row, the choruses on either side, and the instruments above. Directly opposite, and commencing from nearly the top of the great western entrance, was a large compartment of raised seats, corresponding with the orchestra, but of much greater depth; this compartment also, filled up the space between the great pillars. The middle of the nave, or space on the floor between the terminations of the orchestra and the raised seats, was covered with a low platform, on which were ranged three benches. Parts of the north and south aisles were portioned off.

In case there was concern on the part of the readers, the report continued:

> There was but one entrance ... [but] ... No confusion or crowding occurred; the seats were well arranged, easily approached, and very convenient. The prices of admittance the two days were, in the western gallery 12s 6d, to the floor 10s, to the north and south aisles the charge of admission was 3s, an alteration which gave much satisfaction; and as it enabled a large number of persons to enjoy rich musical treats, it reflected great credit on the gentleman under whose directions the arrangements were made.
> The scene during the performance was of uncommon splendour. Our view was taken from the floor. Looking in the direction of the great west

window, the ranks of beauty rising gradually from the floor to the highest row was splendid beyond description; and it was impossible to look around and view the sublime nave, with its grand Norman pillars, and beautifully ribbed and vaulted roof – the performers, both vocal and instrumental, with their animated countenances – the brilliant audience on the raised seats, on the floor, and in the sides – to listen to the pealing of the organ, the harmonising tones of the instruments, and the thrilling sounds of the voices – without feeling that we were in the midst of grandeur and sublimity. We confess that, before we entered the Cathedral, we had our doubts as to the effect of removing the site of the performances from the choir to the nave; we feared there would be reverberations of sound almost totally destructive to harmony; we were, however, delighted to find that our fears had been groundless.

Still to see and be seen

Another description was given in the *Hereford Journal*. There was 'a raised platform in the centre of the Western Aisle' where those who took their 'seats on the raised inclined plane which were so admirably contrived that all could take their places without trouble or confusion, and could' (most importantly at this time) 'see and be seen'. In this period, as was referred to in the previous chapter, there was still a fairly rigid division of taste and accomplishment between the aristocracy and the aspiring middle classes. The growing middle classes of the nineteenth century were either professional musicians, such as those who constituted the Philharmonic Society, or non-participating, more or less affluent bourgeoisie. They favoured English opera and increasingly Haydn, Mozart and Beethoven, and Spohr and Mendelssohn. Only Handel was popular on both sides, as well with the working classes. However, by 1850 the division was on its way out, and by 1850 had largely dissolved.

Complaints and opposition

Unfortunately, not everyone was as impressed as the local reporters. There were firstly complaints that seats had no backs. And the move was apparently not appreciated by some soloists. The seats issue was remedied at least partially by 1855 when it was reported that larger numbers of seats had been provided (including 617 of them with backs) 'because of the great facilities offered by railway communication'. The move into the nave had come just at the right time, with the larger number of tickets being sold across a wider area with the advent of rail services: railways arrived in Gloucester in 1844, Hereford in 1853 and Worcester in 1850. And they certainly resulted in larger crowds attending the Festivals in each city.

Opponents of the Festival – and there were still a considerable number of these through the nineteenth century – saw it as another step on the road to commercialisation. A few years before this, in 1826, one of their number, the social commentator and journalist William Cobbett, travelling through the county on one of his *Rural Rides*, discovered too late that he was trying to get a bed for the night in Gloucester on the first day of that year's Festival:

> But when I came to Gloucester, I found, that I should run a risk of *having no bed* if I did not bow very low and pay very high; for what should there be here, but one of those scandalous and beastly fruits of the system called a 'MUSIC MEETING'. Those who founded the CATHEDRALS never dreamed they would be put to such uses as this! They are, upon these occasions, made use of as *Opera-Houses* ... From this scene of prostitution and of pocket-picking I moved off with all convenient speed ...

And of the concert itself, the *Hereford Times* ...

The local reporter was again impressed. Not with the weather: 'the rain poured down in torrents'. Nevertheless, he reported:

> at 11 o'clock the morning's performances commenced with an audience amounting to 736. Nearly every seat was occupied; and at the beginning of the overture, the nave presented a most splendid spectacle. Caradori, Knyvett, Vaughan and Boisragon, were the principal singers in the first part of that sublime composition, *The Last Judgement*. The treble solo, "Those, who passed through heavy tribulation", &c. was sung admirably by Caradori. In part the second, Phillips sung the recitative "The Day of Wrath is near", in his best style; but the quartet and chorus, "Blest are the departed", was performed in a magnificent manner, the quartet by Mrs Knyvett and Messrs. Knyvett, Vaughan, and Phillips, being one of the most delightful performances of the morning.

Conrad Boisragon, from Cheltenham, was making his Festival debut, having recently made his professional debut in his home town. Under the name Conrado Borrani he later regularly appeared in London opera in the 1840s.

The second part opened with a selection from Haydn's *Creation*:

The first part of this composition we have ever considered the finest, and, therefore, we were gratified at the selection. The introduction [representation of chaos] is one of the sublimest of musical compositions; and the orchestra, led by the veteran Cramer, did justice to the conception of the immortal composer. The chorus, 'Despairing, cursing, rage attends their rapid fall', was most effective. The beautiful air, 'The marv'lous works behold amazed', was sung divinely by Stockhausen, *and this was all she did sing during the whole of the morning's performances.*

Such was the impression of Stockhausen's singing, that we were fearful for the success of Caradori, who immediately followed in a recitative and air; but in the latter, 'With verdure clad the fields appear', Caradori was surpassingly beautiful. Mr Braham in the recitative, 'In splendour height is rising now', seemed to be himself again. 'In native worth and honour clad' was sung by Mr Sapio in a manner that made us regret that he, like Madame Stockhausen, was employed but *once during the whole of the morning's performances'* [italics original]. Mr Knyvett was charming in the sweet air from Handel's 'Judas Maccabaeus', 'From mighty kings he took the spoil'. The highest praise is due to Mr Braham for the manner in which he sung the air, 'Total eclipse! No sun, no moon!' The performances in the Cathedral this morning concluded with a solo and chorus, 'As from the power of sacred lays', from Handel's 'Ode to St Cecilia's Day'.

The Festival at the time

The preoccupation with the soloists and their contributions in the report above demonstrates that they were still the major draw of these festivals, and the local aristocracy the target audience. By this time the Festivals had settled into a regular pattern, with an opening service in the cathedral on the first (Wednesday) morning and oratorio performances on the two subsequent ones, and a concert and ball in a secular venue each evening.

Maria Caradori-Allan (1800–65), the Italian-born soprano who settled in England and had her first London debut in 1822. Hand-coloured lithograph by Henri Grevedon, 1831 (© National Portrait Gallery, London)

While the three cathedrals' choirs still formed the backbone of the chorus, members were also increasingly being recruited from elsewhere, in particular from the northern choral societies. It had long been the practice to draw on orchestral players from the capital. Francois Cramer as usual led the band for the morning performances, sharing his duties in the evening with J.D. Loder and Nicholas Mori, while the names of many of the leading players of the day are to be found among the other performers. In all, 10 principal singers were employed, 71 instrumentalists and 119 choralists, making a total of 200 performers in 1834.

At the following year's Festival in Gloucester the orchestra, now with more space to grow into, consisted of 24 violins, ten violas, six cellos, six double basses 'with wind in proportion' and the players were drawn 'from the Concert of Ancient Music, Philharmonic, Italian Opera and other establishments in London'.

S.S. Wesley

S.S. Wesley, who oversaw this revolution, was an ambitious young musician, who had been appointed organist at Hereford Cathedral just a couple of years earlier, in 1832. However, he was already regretting moving from London where his early compositions had been performed and where he had seemed set to embark on a career as an organist and composer, and entitled to expect further successes in the theatre and concert hall.

Hereford then was a sleepy country market town with a population of little more than a third of Camberwell, which Wesley was familiar with. The move was one he was to bitterly regret in later life, and there can be little doubt that had he known the reality of life at a provincial cathedral he would have thought long and hard about leaving the capital. Encouragement, one suspects, had come from the new dean of Hereford, the ambitious Dr John Merewether, who had previously been curate of Hampton parish church, where Wesley had recently been evening organist. It was Dr Merewether who had supported the move into the nave.

Wesley later recalled, when looking back over his career:

> Painful and dangerous is the position of the young musician who, after acquiring great knowledge of his art in the Metropolis, joins a country Cathedral. At first he can scarcely believe that the mass of error and inferiority in which he has to participate is habitual and irremediable. He thinks he will reform matters, gently, and without giving offence: but he soon discovers that it is his approbation and not his advice that is needed. The choir is 'the best in England', (such being the belief at most Cathedrals) and, if he give trouble in his attempts at improvement, he would be, by some Chapters, at once voted a person with whom they 'cannot go on smoothly', and 'a bore'.

Wesley and the 1834 Festival as a whole

Wesley's first contact with the Festival had been in 1833 when he had acted as pianist at the Worcester meeting, accompanying the solo items at the secular evening concerts. But his thoughts had turned to the subject of his home Festival debut as early as December 1832 when in a reference to an instrumentalist's employment at a future festival he informed him that, 'The Dean intends to <u>rouse the world!</u> [writer's emphasis] And bring it here.' Another plan had been to invite his father to come and conduct his setting of Psalm 111, *Confitebor Tibi Domine* but this fell through due to his father's age and infirmity. The violinist was appointed, though, for 15 guineas.

While individual soloists chose their own solo items, ultimate responsibility for the programme – subject to the approval of the stewards – lay with Wesley. The beginnings of a move from over-dependence on the music of Handel had been felt two years earlier when John Amott, newly appointed to Gloucester, had included a selection from Spohr's *The Last Judgement*, Neukomm's *Mount*

S.S. Wesley (1810–76), leading English organist and composer, whose lengthy career included holding the organist posts of Hereford Cathedral, Exeter Cathedral, Leeds Parish Church, Winchester Cathedral and Gloucester Cathedral in turn

Sinai and Mozart's *Requiem* in his programme. But it fell to Wesley (who had a particular fondness for the work) to offer a complete performance of *The Last Judgement*. To allow time for both this and a complete performance of Mozart's *Requiem*, only a selection from *Messiah* was included. 'This departure from all precedent', Amott later observed in the *Annals*, 'has ... never been repeated, and, it is hoped, never will be'. There was more Spohr on offer in the evening concerts, with performances of the overture to *Jessonda* and an extended selection from *Azor und Zemira* which had first been heard in England in 1831 in an adaptation by Sir George Smart at Covent Garden.

The appeal of Spohr

Wesley was a career-long admirer of Spohr's music, later in his life passing on to the young Hubert Parry the opinion that Spohr, 'excelled ... because he could bring such a marvellous tone out of his orchestra'. Spohr had begun composing *The Last Judgement* in October 1825 and finished it in time to perform it with his choral society in Kassel on Good Friday 1826. Following its first appearances at the Three Choirs, it was subsequently a regular item on Festival programmes until 1901, after which it disappeared without trace. Other works by Spohr were also regular features of the Festival during this time. Nineteenth-century opinion was that Spohr was a great composer, and considered his oratorio *The Last Judgement* a masterpiece. It reportedly overwhelmed its early audiences and remained popular until the First World War, when it sank into obscurity, only comparatively recently being reassessed and performed again. Spohr was a pivotal composer, sometimes too indebted to his predecessors, while his successors tended to improve upon his innovations. Experts detect in *The Last Judgement* passages reminiscent of Mozart's *Magic Flute* and Beethoven's *Fidelio*, while its brooding orchestration and muscular choral writing anticipate the work of Schumann and Brahms.

Mozart was the other composer best represented at the 1834 Three Choirs with the overture to *Don Giovani* and the second half of the finale to Act 1 of *Cosi fan tutti* in addition to the *Requiem* and various operatic arias. From Wesley himself there were: an overture (probably one that he had hoped to perform at Covent Garden in 1833), a *Benedictus*, framed by choral settings of the *Sanctus* and *Osanna* (now lost) and the canzonet *When we two were parted* and a sacred song with orchestral accompaniment, *Abraham's Offering*. The first performance of the latter was entrusted to an old friend of Wesley's from the English Opera House, Henry Phillips, who it appears hadn't had much rehearsal time: 'Mr Phillipps [sic] was evidently new to the subject, which circumstance was much against the effect of the performance', as the *Hereford Times* later reported.

Writing to his mother some four weeks after the Festival, Wesley was able to report to her that he had been spoken very highly of in the *Hereford Journal*. It reported:

To Mr S.S. Wesley ... no common praise is due – deprived of those benefits which a long residence amongst us would have imparted in appreciating the public taste, his selections have given general satisfaction; the musical departments were ably filled, and the noble band greatly surpassed that of any former meeting – the talents selected, vocal and instrumental, were first rate, and most creditable to his judgement.

Inside Worcester Cathedral during the 1848 Festival (© The British Library Board)

3

Hubert Parry

Gloucester Cathedral: 8 September 1868

At the 1.30pm concert on 8 September 1868 Hubert Parry made his Three Choirs Festival composer's debut with a short orchestral piece called Intermezzo Religioso. *It was in a programme that also included the first part of Haydn's* Creation, *Beethoven's* Mass in C, *Mendelssohn's setting of Psalm 42 and Samuel Wesley's* Confitebor Tibi, Domine.

THE CONCERT, AND the 1868 Festival itself, was directed by Samuel Sebastian Wesley, the Gloucester organist. Little had changed since his time directing the Festivals as Hereford Cathedral organist in the 1830s. It now always spanned four days, with the opening service (sung by the combined cathedral choirs) on the Tuesday morning, and the concluding performance of Handel's *Messiah* and evening ball the following Friday. The orchestra was still largely composed of professionals from London, while the chorus included the cathedral choirs and the recently-formed choral societies from the three cities as well as contingents from elsewhere in the country. The musical forces had continued to grow, and Wesley was now responsible for organising a body of over 300 instrumentalists and singers.

Widespread criticism

The Festival was in a rut, and criticism of it was widespread from music critics, as this extract from *Musical World* just after this Festival demonstrates:

The English composer, teacher and writer Sir (Charles) Hubert Hastings Parry (1848–1918) (© National Portrait Gallery, London)

It is easy to understand the reasons why these Festivals secure so much attention, but difficult to associate it in any way with music. As a matter of fact, the value of the Festivals, from an art point of view, is of the smallest. That ought not to be, but that it must needs be, so long as a local organist fills the conductor's seat, is obvious. Nothing more absurd can be imagined. Messrs Wesley, Done and Smith are doubtless very respectable in the places they legitimately occupy; but it is one thing to accompany *Boyce in A* and another to conduct a full orchestra. It would scarcely be fair to blame those gentlemen for the results, insomuch as bound to do their best they do it. Unfortunately, the degree in which they are energetic is precisely the degree in which they work mischief. Here we can imagine nothing better for the Festivals than a total want of energy on the part of the organist. Messrs Wesley, Done and [George Townsend] Smith, baton in hand, resolved to use it with a vigour, are the most powerful enemies those festivals can have. The devotion and duty of the Gloucester conductor was, therefore, calculated to excite mingled admiration and regret. For the sake of Dr Wesley we could not have wished it less, but for the sake of the music we could cheerfully have dispensed with it.

Two of the morning programmes being, as a matter of course, taken up by *Elijah* and the *Messiah*, the managers seemed to have resolved upon crowding into the other two as many works as possible.

The crowding-in resulted in over-long concerts that tested the resolve of audience, critics and performers.

Another contemporary professional music critic, Joseph Bennett, when looking back on this period from the perspective of the early years of the twentieth century, was more circumspect:

[He remembered William Done as a] good amiable man [who] was as feebly built as a suburban villa, but Smith had strength. The orchestra would follow him without any sense of risk; he knew what he wanted and generally got it ... with Done, Townsend Smith and Wesley the orchestra was always on good terms ... Done was not properly speaking a conductor at all, but he was a gentle, amiable man, and the London players steered him through

Inside Gloucester Shire Hall during a secular concert at the 1853 Festival
(© The British Library Board)

many a difficult passage. On his part Smith, the best conductor of the three, was recognised as such and followed; while Wesley, more distinctly a non-conductor than even Done, commanded respect by his high musicianship and brilliant achievements as a composer and organist.

Youngest Oxford music graduate: Hubert Parry

On his way to becoming one of the country's leading classical musicians and administrators, Parry at this time was a student at Exeter College Oxford, reading Law and Modern History. His father had ambitions of a commercial career for him, but Parry was thoroughly engaged with the musical life of the University. Earlier, while still at Eton, he had successfully sat the Oxford Bachelor of Music examination, the youngest person ever to have done so. His examination exercise, a cantata, *O Lord, Thou hast cast us out*, reportedly 'astonished' the assessors and was performed and published in 1867.

He was the third and second surviving son of Thomas Gambier Parry, a distinguished artist, amateur musician, collector of *objets d'art,* local benefactor and supporter and sometime steward of the Three Choirs Festival,

A Festival garden party at Highnam Court in 1910
(photograph © Ian Russell, Shulbrede Priory Parry Archive)

who had bought the seventeenth-century country house Highnam Court near Gloucester in 1837. Hubert was born in 1848, his mother's sixth child who died giving birth to him. Gambier Parry therefore had been left to raise three young children on his own. He himself had been orphaned at the age of five when his mother, Mary, died. Gambier Parry's father, and Hubert Parry's grandfather, Richard Parry, had enjoyed a distinguished career in the civil service, spending much of his professional life in India. Two years after returning to England in 1813, his election to a directorship of the notorious East India Company, like his father before him, assured him of greater wealth. But he died in 1817. His own father, Thomas Parry, had died in 1816, leaving much of his wealth to his namesake and only grandson, Thomas Gambier Parry, who was born two months before his death. This inherited wealth enabled the purchase of Highnam Court and the lifestyle that went with the ownership of a country seat.

Early in his childhood, Hubert started playing the organ at the church his father had built for Highnam village, and his diary records how in his teens he spent many happy days during the holidays trying the organs in the neighbourhood, noting their qualities, specifications, and the names of their makers. He also recruited the organist of the church, Edward Brind, for lessons in piano, harmony and counterpoint, and Brind in turn sought to broaden the young Parry's horizons, taking him to the Hereford Festival of 1861 with its heady diet of massed choir, orchestra and the music of Spohr, Mendelssohn and Handel. He also began composing while at Eton, his first known piece being a set of *Variegations* [sic] for piano which he composed in 1862.

The debut piece

The *Intermezzo Religioso* originated as the slow movement of a Sonata for piano duet in F minor that Parry had composed, among other works, in the Michaelmas Term of 1865 when laid up in the Eton School Sanatorium having been knocked virtually unconscious during a football match. The sonata was 'tentative, structurally unambitious, and extremely Mendelssohnian' according to Parry expert Jeremy Dibble. But Parry had showed it to his private music tutor and it became a scoring exercise. At that time Parry was, on the advice of Wesley, studying orchestration with Henry Hugo Pierson, formerly Reid Professor of Music at the University of Edinburgh, then living in Stuttgart, Germany.

Master and protégé: Wesley and Parry

Parry's Festival debut, and his time with Pierson, were the result of a growing friendship with S.S. Wesley. They had first met in Winchester while Parry was a pupil at Twyford School, and now, with Parry back home at Highnam Court and Wesley the newly-appointed organist of Gloucester Cathedral, their paths crossed again. As a close acquaintance of Parry's father, Wesley became a regular visitor to Highnam, which provided opportunity for Parry to quiz him, particularly on the subject of instrumentation. Parry's then-teacher, George Elvey, was much more conservative than Wesley, and Parry had grown impatient with him.

During the Easter vacation of 1865, Parry was invited to sing in a choral concert in Gloucester Cathedral which was to include a performance of his setting of Shakespeare's *Take, O take those lips away* for four-part male-voice choir, written in February for his father's birthday. It also included the first local performance of Wesley's *Ode to Labour*, Sterndale Bennett's *The May*

Queen, Mendelssohn's *Die Lorelei* and a selection of other part songs. After a rehearsal on 17 April Parry noted in his diary:

> We had a full-dress rehearsal in the evening conducted by Sterndale Bennett and Wesley. The things we rehearsed were Professor Sterndale Bennett's 'May Queen', Dr Wesley's 'Ode', Mendelssohn's 'Lorelei' and some part songs. I had to conduct my own.

After the event, Parry wrote:

> Had rehearsal again at 12. The 'Ode' was the chief thing we had to practise. I had luncheon at the Palace, and went afterwards to the cathedral and played the voluntary. Dr Wesley gave me leave to play there whenever I like ... In the evening we had the concert ... Some parts of Wesley's Ode are quite magnificent, especially the first bass solo, which is as fine as anything I have heard of the kind ... My little part song ... Though not having had enough rehearsal ... Dr Wesley positively sang bass in it: it went better the second time ...

Attending the 1865 Gloucester Festival, Parry was impressed and later wrote ecstatically of Mendelssohn's *Elijah* and *Die erste Walpurgisnacht*, and declared *Messiah* 'the greatest music ever conceived'. He was critical of Wesley's conducting, considering his tempo too fast, but enthused over his superb fugal improvisation on the organ.

During the following year, 1866, Parry's five-part madrigal *Fair Daffodils* was publicly performed for the first time in Gloucester – 'very badly', he wrote in his diary – before later being performed at the Royal Glee and Madrigal Union, and at the Eton College Musical Society spring concert in 1866.

Wesley had taken the young Parry under his wing, boosting his confidence by participating in the performance of his part song, as well as allowing him the freedom of the cathedral organ, which Parry later described as 'a grand old instrument in a very bad state, but with a sort of glorious richness about it'. And in the Easter vacation of 1867 there was a performance in the cathedral of Parry's BMus cantata, *O Lord though hast cast us out*. Wesley

THE GLOUCESTER MUSICAL FESTIVAL: THE CLERESTORY, GLOUCESTER CATHEDRAL.

SOUTH PORCH, GLOUCESTER CATHEDRAL.

ILLUSTRATIONS OF THE GLOUCESTER MUSICAL FESTIVAL.

THE proceedings at the 142nd Festival of the Three Choirs of Gloucester, Worcester, and Hereford, which took place at Gloucester from Tuesday, the 5th, to Friday, the 8th inst., were sufficiently described in our last. The sacred music was performed each day in the cathedral; the evening concerts of secular music, ending with a ball, were of course relegated to the Shirehall. It is from the cathedral performances that we have chosen the subjects for the Illustrations we have engraved this week. One is an exterior view, showing the South Porch of that venerable edifice, with the crowd which daily assembled in front of it, keeping, however, a portion of the thoroughfare open for the entrance and departure of the company. This porch—a very fine specimen of English Perpendicular architecture—was built about the year 1420, by Abbot Morwent, to whose work belongs also that portion of the nave, looking westward,

shown in another of our present Illustrations. The porch has an upper chamber, and side windows of peculiar tracery, the mullions of which continue the arrangement of the panelling of the walls; it is supported by buttresses at the angles, and surmounted with pinnacles rising from an open parapet, the whole enriched with niches and canopies; the arms of England, France, and Gloucester Abbey sculptured in the spandrils of the doorway.

The nave, of which our Artist has furnished a View, with the audience or congregation which thronged its benches on the days of the musical festival, is materially different from those of most other Norman cathedrals in England; the lofty and massive piers being carried so high as to leave the triforium a comparatively small space, instead of its being, as at Norwich, Ely, and Peterborough, nearly equal in dimensions to the nave-arcade below.

The large window at the west end was erected, at the expense of the Rev. Canon T. M. Brown, as a memorial of the late Bishop Monk. The design represents various incidents of Old and New Testament

history; it is the work of Mr. Wailes. We may take this opportunity of stating that five additional stained windows have just been placed in the nave of Gloucester Cathedral. A sixth is now being prepared by Clayton and Bell, and when this is fixed, of all the many windows of the nave there will remain only one that has not been furnished with stained glass. The artists whose studios are represented are Clayton and Bell, Hardman, Wailes, Ward, and Hughes, Preedy, Warrington, and Bell, of Bristol. The four new windows are intended, respectively, as memorials of the late Mr. J. Elliott, solicitor, Mrs. Price, and the relatives of the Rev. Sir Lionel Darrell; but two of the windows are restorations, by Mr. Hardman, for which the public are indebted to the Dean and Chapter, while the taste and liberality which have led to the erection of the memorials have, to a great extent, been initiated and stimulated by Mr. W. V. Ellis, who, though himself not a member of the Established Church, devotes unceasing trouble and much time and money to the decoration of this cathedral.

The clerestory, in which a number of ladies and gentlemen found

Scenes inside and outside Gloucester Cathedral during the 1865 Festival
(© The British Library Board)

then agreed to include Parry's *Intermezzo Religioso* in the next Gloucester Festival due the following year. A big step up for Parry's burgeoning career.

The context: the Festival of 1868

In the run up to the Festival, Wesley's preparations included visits to London, among them his first visit to the Crystal Palace to hear Schubert's *Symphony No.9* (14 December 1867) recommended to him by George Grove. He was also spotted at one of Boosey's Ballad Concerts in early April, no doubt to meet Charlotte Sainton-Dolby who was subsequently engaged as principal contralto. Sims Reeves, Therese Tietjens and Charles Santley were also engaged – as principal tenor, soprano and bass respectively. In his choice of oratorios for the programme, Wesley again stuck with Handel, Mendelssohn and Spohr, together with Weber's little known *Praise Jehovah* (an adaptation of *Jubel-Kantate*) and two contemporary works – Gounod's *Messe Solennelle* (1855) and Schachner's *The Return of Israel from Babylon* (1862), first considered for the 1865 Festival.

In one respect the Festival differed considerably from the previous Gloucester one in 1865, as the experiment then of placing the chorus and orchestra at the west end was not repeated. Also, with the stewards anxious to avoid the cost of an extra instrument, Wesley had agreed to try to use the cathedral organ. Though this proved impossible, and an organ incorporating the new electropneumatic action, enabling the console to be placed in the orchestra, was hired from Bryceson Brothers. At the opening service on 8 September, Bach's motet *Blessing, glory, wisdom and thanks* was performed and Canon Lysons preached.

The famous English tenor, (John) Sims Reeves (1818–1900) by Alessandro Ossani, 1863 (© National Portrait Gallery, London)

A mixed bag: the concert

Held shortly after the opening service, on Tuesday at 1.30pm, Parry's *Intermezzo Religioso* took its place in a concert alongside the first part of Haydn's *Creation,* Beethoven's *Mass in C,* Mendelssohn's setting of Psalm 42, and Wesley's father's setting of Psalm 111, *Confitebor Tibi, Domine.* In so far as keeping programmes to a reasonable length, Wesley had learnt nothing from his earlier experiences, or from criticism from visitors and the press. Beethoven's *Mass in C* suffered from a lack of rehearsal time as the *Annals* records:

[An] unfortunate breakdown at the commencement of the Kyrie owing to the uncertainty of the tempo adopted, created an uneasy feeling that more disasters were in store, and by the time Miss Edith Wynne came in with her solo hopeless confusion reigned supreme, so that the movement came to a sudden collapse and was re-commenced. To atone for this disaster the soloists appeared to vie with each other in bringing out the beautiful points of the succeeding numbers, which were all admirably rendered. Mendelssohn's 42nd Psalm, with the solo sung by Mdlle Tietjens, brought the morning's performance to an end.

The character of a dirge: a mixed response

The performance of Parry's debut work elicited only a muted response from the audience. Among the better critiques was one written by the *The Musical Standard* reporter who described his work as 'a most charming orchestral composition by a highly accomplished young amateur'. However, from one London daily newspaper, the *Standard,* it provoked some invective:

> No key to the composer's intentions was published in the programme. It may be assumed that between Haydn and Samuel Wesley there is some intermediate stage, and that between the *Creation* and the Psalm it was necessary that the mind should be relieved by a kind of voluntary executed by full orchestra. If it had been playing out of a congregation any intermezzo would suffice, and that of Hubert Parry would have received as much attention as is ordinarily paid to voluntaries after long sermons. The movement of the intermezzo itself has the character of a dirge; it opens with a grave strain from the strings, and the ear catches for a moment some Spohrish characters in the sound, the oboe having a prominent place therein, and then a kind of Mendelssohnian subject, languid and undulating, winds up the piece, the workmanship of which is creditable, but the invention of which is not exciting, and the whole had the sin of being thrust in the programme where it was not wanted.

Ten days later Parry called on Wesley, whom he found 'very amusing on the subject of the Festival & the Critics thereon' and who told him that the writer, Gruneisen, had a grudge against the Gloucester Festival and

THE FESTIVAL OF THE THREE CHOIRS IN WORCESTER CATHEDRAL.—SEE PRECEDING PAGE.

'wants to do all the harm he can'. George Grove, meanwhile (to whom Parry was introduced for the first time through the efforts of Arthur Sullivan), attempted to console him with the advice that abuse was 'a good sign'.

Other reports were more encouraging. *The Musical World* described how, 'A novelty in the morning programme was an 'intermezzo religioso' by Mr Hubert Parry, which in no way belies its amateur origin'.

In a letter to his girlfriend, Maud Herbert, soon after, Parry wrote:

> The Festival was altogether successful; some of the music went better than ever, and the singers sang sometimes almost better than they perhaps thought they were capable of doing ... I was complemented on the little *Intermezzo* a good deal by all the swell musicians who were down here, and some of them congratulated me more especially on its not being very highly approved of by some of the newspaper critics, as that is always said to be a good sign. I believe the 'Guardian' critic will be kind to me, but his criticism will not come out till next week; if you see it ever, look and see if he abuses me ...

The *Gloucestershire Chronicle* of 19 September quoted *The Guardian*:

> *The Guardian* contains an able critique of the week's performance written, we believe, by Prof Oakley of Edinburgh. Speaking of the work composed by Mr Hubert Parry Mus Bac, the writer says – 'This work was, we believe, designed when the young composer was at Eton, and was scored last year when he was studying at Stuttgard under Mr H. Hugh Pierson, who for a short time held the professorship of music at the University of Edinburgh. The *Intermezzo* consists of one movement, Andante in A flat, and evinces throughout refined taste and musician-like feeling. After some thirty bars – the fifth and sixth of which seem to show the fascinating influence of Mendelssohn – a transition is made to the relative minor, and the first and second violins give out in octaves a graceful phrase in crotchets, to which the violas make flowing and effective semiquaver accompaniment. A return is then made to a second subject lately heard in a dominant key,

Inside Worcester Cathedral during the 1866 Festival (© The British Library Board)

which on its reappearance is introduced, according to the correct form, in the tonic, and a few bars later, the opening phrase recurs, when the organ pedal is effectively brought in. The movement, which is very short, ends with a few bars of reminiscences and quotation of some of the preceding subjects. It would have been better appreciated by the audience as well as critics had greater pains been taken with its performance. The talent of which the composer has given such an early indication deserves far more recognition and encouragement than that accorded to it last week.

Overall responses to the Festival

Like most people, Parry struggled with the length of some of the concerts and reported in his diary that the Thursday morning performance:

was the most remarkably lengthy affair I ever had the felicity to sit through; it began at 11.30 and ended about 5.15 (with half an hour for lunch); and as might have been anticipated for the last half hour or so a complete lassitude took possession of everyone concerned; the principal singers gave up the ghost and sang miserably, the Orchestra simply collapsed, and the chorus were incapable of the exertion of singing & the audience yet more incapable of listening.

The audience fared no better in the evening, with a programme that lasted from 7.45pm until 11.15pm, and both Parry and the critic of *The Musical Standard* left before the end.

Although the week had its share of mishaps, most notably the (unrehearsed) opening of Beethoven's *Mass in C* breaking down, there was fairly general agreement that the Festival had been a success. Parry particularly enjoyed Spohr's *Die Heilands letze Stunden, Elijah,* and Handel's *Messiah,* and, at the evening concerts, Mendelssohn's *Hebrides Overture,* the selection from *Don Giovanni,* and Sullivan's new orchestral song *I wish to tune my quivering lyre,* while *The Musical Standard* praised the performances of Beethoven's *Symphony No.5* and Mendelssohn's *Lobgesang.* Yet as might have been expected, there was carping from some quarters. Wesley's old adversary Charles Gruneisen, writing in *The Standard,* still had nothing positive to say, while the *Pall Mall Gazette,* as quoted earlier, declared that:

the value of the Festivals, from an art point of view, is of the smallest. This ought not to be, but that it needs be, so long as a local organist fills the conductor's seat is obvious ... There were however, points of excellence which not even Dr. Wesley could spoil.

A lasting relationship: Parry at the Festival

After this initial appearance, Parry continued to visit and support the Festival through his distinguished musical career, latterly as director of the Royal College of Music. He is known to have been present at the 1874 Festival in Gloucester, where he met George Grove and Sir John Stainer, and also the one in 1877. He also made a generous gift that facilitated an extension to Gloucester's Shire Hall concert hall in time for the 1910 Festival, and he hosted regular social events for performers during the Gloucester Festival weeks. During the 1922 Festival, the first Gloucester Festival following his death in 1918, a memorial plaque to him was unveiled in Gloucester by Viscount Gladstone, a friend of Parry's from his Eton days. Also present were Elgar, Stanford, Granville Bantock, Sir Hugh Allen (Parry's successor as director of the Royal College of Music) and the musicologist and educational reformer, Sir Henry Hadow. The ceremony concluded with a moving performance of *Blest Pair of Sirens* conducted by Sir Hugh Allen, who refused to start until every choir member's copy had been thrown to the ground. And at the 1925 Festival, Sir Hugh Allen unveiled a memorial tablet to Parry at the Shire Hall during the interval of the evening concert there.

The *Intermezzo Religioso* proved to be the first of a long series of works which Parry wrote over a period of something like 45 years for the Three Choirs and other festivals. Inspiration was bound to fail sometimes, but some of his finest works were produced at Gloucester Festivals as first performances, including the one he was commissioned to write for the 1880 Festival, *Prometheus Unbound*.

Prometheus Unbound

Parry chose as his text the radical ideology of Shelley's *Prometheus Unbound* – a work to which he had been recently attracted. But the first performance was fraught with difficulties and frustrations for the composer. The orchestral parts were late in arriving and were then found to be full of mistakes, and for Parry:

> the rehearsal exceeded my worst expectations. We were so driven for time
> that in most cases we could only go straight through and call attention to
> mistakes in the execution and trust to 'Provy' for their being rectified in
> the performance.

The orchestra had already been rehearsing for seven or eight hours and 'though they tried their best it was as much as they could do to keep their attention to it'. In addition, the 250-strong chorus, drawn from the three cathedral cities and also London, Bristol, Oxford and Huddersfield, was bewildered by the work. However, matters improved the following day when a large company of chorus members from Huddersfield arranged a private rehearsal and lifted the general morale of the choir. Parry was touched by this and later reported that they 'got together of their own free will and had a private rehearsal under their own chorus master without telling me till just before the performance, and the result was astonishing'.

The performance itself, despite several awkward moments, went surprisingly well in the circumstances, but the general reception of the work was mixed. Some critics immediately took a dislike to it because they detected the strong presence of Wagner, and secondly because they objected to Shelley's atheistic philosophy. Others were more constructively critical.

This piece and its performance in the 1880 Festival has been viewed by many scholars of British music as the most convenient starting point when discussing the so-called English musical Renaissance. But although full of striking ideas, Parry expert Jeremy Dibble believes that:

> the association of the revolutionary vision and intellect of Shelley and
> Parry's apparent literary temerity has tended to blind commentators
> to the cantata's purely musical quality ... although *Prometheus* is full of
> potentially striking ideas ... one soon becomes uncomfortably conscious
> that the Handelian and Mendelssohnian conditioning of Parry's early
> musical training and experience of English choral festivals lurks just
> beneath the surface ...

As Gustav Holst later said:

1880 is usually given as the date of the 'modern Renaissance' in English music. For me it began about 20 years later when I first knew Elgar's *Enigma Variations*. I felt that here was music the like of which had not appeared in this country since Purcell's death.

Parry brought a further 13 new works to the Festivals during the rest of his life. These were, *Glories of our Blood and State* (1883), *Suite Moderne* (1886), *De Profundis* (1891), *Job* (1892), *Overture to an Unwritten Tragedy* (1893), *Magnificat* (1897), *A Song of Darkness and Light* (1898), *Thanksgiving Te Deum in F* (1900), *Voces Clamantium* (1903), *The Love that Casteth out Fear* (1904), *The Soul's Ransom* (1906), *Beyond These Voices* (1908) and *Ode on the Nativity of Christ* (1912). Clearly, the Festival couldn't get enough of him, or he the Festival. Or he just couldn't say no. Jaeger, of Novello's, the publishers, knew it was the latter. When the Gloucester committee approached Parry for a new work for the 1904 Festival he wrote to the composer:

I feel almost inclined to commiserate with you, because those kind Gloucester people want another *new* work. Let them do the splendid *Te Deum* and allow you to devote your time to clear up arrears ... a little! Why not? Why *won't* they leave you alone for once and give you rest?

4

Female composers

Shire Hall, Hereford: 12 September 1882

On 12 September 1882, the first known performance of a piece of music by a female composer was heard at a Three Choirs Festival. Alice Mary Smith's Ode to the Passions *appeared on the programme of the Tuesday evening secular concert in Hereford's Shire Hall. During the final chamber concert, on 15 September, a song,* From my Sad Tears are Springing (Aus meinen Thränen)*, by another leading nineteenth-century female composer, Rosalind Ellicott, was also performed by herself, a keen and talented singer. Whereas Smith made no further Festival appearances, Ellicott went on to have a number of premieres over the next several years. Neither was invited to conduct, as male composers of new works regularly were. That had to wait for the new century, and the next generation of composers.*

Favourably known to the musical world: Alice Mary Smith

A LSO KNOWN AS Mrs Meadows White – Frederick Meadows White, her husband, was a lawyer and later a judge – Alice Mary Smith was a highly-regarded and prolific composer at this time. The programme notes for the 1882 concert referred to the fact that she was 'favourably known to the musical world of London'. And according to an obituary published after her sudden death in 1884:

> Her music is marked by elegance and grace ... power and energy. Her forms were always clear and her ideas free from eccentricity; her sympathies were evidently with the Classic rather than with the Romantic school.

Rosalind Ellicott (1857–1924) was one of the leading female composers of her generation. Portrait by Herbert Rose Barraud, 1890 (© National Portrait Gallery)

Alice Mary Smith (1839–84) was a prolific composer, writing for a diverse range of ensembles. She was also known under her married name of Mrs Meadows White

Born in 1839, she had shown an aptitude for music from childhood and took private lessons from leading music educators of the day, Sterndale Bennett and George Macfarren. She had her first song published in 1857, and ten years later was elected Female Professional Associate of the Royal Philharmonic Society. By the time contact was made with the Festival in 1882, Smith was a prolific composer writing for a diverse range of ensembles. Among her chamber compositions were four piano quartets, three string quartets and a clarinet sonata (1870). Her orchestral compositions included six concert overtures and two symphonies. Her first symphony, in C minor, was written at the age of 24 and performed by the Musical Society of London in 1863; the first known symphony by a female composer to be performed. The second, in A minor, was written for the Alexandra Palace competition of 1876, but was never submitted.

Smith also composed two large pieces for the stage: an operetta, which was performed in 1865 at the Fitzwilliam Music Society, Cambridge, and *The Masque of Pandora* (1875), for which the orchestration was never completed. Smith's output also includes one of the largest collections of sacred choral music by a woman composer, and comprises six anthems, three canticles (and the beginning to a fourth), as well as a short Sacred Cantata *Exile*, based on episodes from Jean Racine's *Esther*. Two of her anthems were performed in a liturgical context, sung by Sir Joseph Barnby's choir of St Andrew's, Wells Street, in February 1864, making them the first recorded instance of music by a female composer being used in the liturgies of the Church of England.

In 1880 she turned her attention towards writing large-scale cantatas, all published by Novello and Co. In 1880 she composed and had published *Ode to the North-East Wind* for chorus and orchestra (1880). Her next was the *Ode to the passions.*

Clever and thoughtful works for the orchestra

It is not clear whether *Ode to the passions* was a commission from the Festival or whether Smith submitted it for consideration. My belief is that it was the latter. But the programme does claim that it was 'composed especially for this festival'. The programme also states, presumably drafted by Alice or her husband, that 'the authoress of the present setting has written many clever and thoughtful works for the orchestra'. It is known, however, that Alice's husband Frederick, an enthusiastic champion of her career, wrote to Sir Theodore Martin, a confidante of Queen Victoria at Buckingham Palace, asking whether the queen might accept the work being dedicated to her. This plan came to nothing as the reply from Martin was, 'the Queen has to be very chary about allowing works to be dedicated to her, otherwise the world would be inundated with applications which it would be too difficult to decline'.

There was also correspondence prior to the Festival as to whether Smith herself should conduct the work. She sought the advice of William Alexander Barrett, a noted critic, on this point. He encouraged her to take it on:

> It would be nice to see a lady conduct on such an occasion, especially one
> who is not altogether unknown. [Langdon] Colborne [the then organist
> of Hereford] is nervous by disposition but conscientious and trustworthy.
> But – this is without prejudice if you wish for a brilliant reading it will be
> necessary for you to conduct yourself.

If she felt unable to do that, he went on to suggest C.H. Lloyd, the Gloucester organist, if she wanted a diplomatic replacement for Colborne. Tact won the day and Colborne conducted, presumably completely unaware of the behind-the-scenes machinations. My thoughts are that it would not have occurred to Colborne that she could conduct it or even want to, even though she was the composer.

Ode to the passions

The *Ode* is a setting of a poem, *The Passions,* by William Collins (1721–59). Known when a student at Oxford University as being 'distinguished for his genius and indolence', Collins moved to London as a young man, but received little encouragement for his writing and was often in debt. When the publication of the *Ode* failed like the others, he bought up most of the remaining copies and destroyed them and became depressed. Latterly he was cared for by his elder sister. However, within his lifetime the *Ode* was set to music by William Hayes in 1750, and after his death was recited by David Garrick. Whilst contemporary opinion of his poetry was that it was contrived, the *Ode* was rated more highly.

Following Hayes' setting, it was also set to music by the organist of Westminster Abbey, Benjamin Cooke, in 1774 and by others. The Hayes version was revived by the Three Choirs Festival in 1760 in Gloucester. Alice Mary Smith's version is in ten movements and set for two soprano, contralto, tenor and bass soloists with chorus and orchestra.

A graceful composer

The concert was held on Tuesday evening, 12 September 1882, in Hereford's Shire Hall, and Smith and her husband stayed as guests of the dean of the cathedral following it. The concert opened with Beethoven's *Egmont Overture* and this was followed by the *Ode.* The second half consisted of Cherubini's overture *Les Deux Journées,* a violin solo, and various vocal solos and ensembles.

The main soloists in the *Ode* were Miss Anna Williams (soprano), Mr Frederick King (baritone) and Mr Frank Boyle (tenor). These were all top names. Anna Williams was a favourite of the festival circuit, and often appeared at the Three Choirs. She later taught at the Royal College of Music. Frederick King was also an established festival singer, who also taught at the Royal Academy of Music, while Frank Boyle was a singer in the D'Oyly Carte Opera Company.

George Robertson Sinclair conducting the chorus in Hereford's Shire Hall
during the 1903 Festival (courtesy of Derek Foxton)

The other soloists in the *Ode* were Marian Fenna (soprano) and Hilda
Wilson (contralto). The orchestra was led by John Tiplady Carrodus, one
of the principal violinists in the north of England, and the choir combined members of the three cathedral choirs and 52 selected members of
the Bradford chorus and other singers, local and from elsewhere, including
members of the Gloucester, Worcester and Hereford choral societies. The
conductor was Langdon Colborne, organist of Hereford Cathedral 1877 to
1889. Although conscientious, he was not considered the most competent of
conductors, as inferred above and as this report in *Society* magazine after the
Festival demonstrates:

> Moderately good performances of familiar works like the *Messiah*, the
> *Elijah* and *Judas Maccabeus* under a conductor by no means used to his
> work, cannot excite any general interest. As to the system of making it a
> rule that the cathedral organist, competent or not, must act as conductor,
> it appears to me to be an outrageously foolish one.

The concert was not particularly well-attended, and, according to a contemporary report, the audience 'took as lively an interest in the proceedings as a defunct person does in his own burial rites'. Even Beethoven's *Egmont* Overture 'fell rather listlessly upon the ears of a not over demonstrative audience'. As the second half of the programme was entirely devoted to solo and chamber items; it was perhaps an unfortunate setting for Smith's work with its large forces. This poor programming decision could perhaps go some way to explain the lacklustre response of the audience.

However, the official *Annals* report of the evening does suggest some enthusiasm:

> the chief feature of the first concert in the shire hall was the production of an *Ode to the Passions* set to music by Mrs Meadows White, known as a graceful composer under her maiden name of Alice Mary Smith. The cantata was well performed, and in obedience to unanimous recall, the composer was led forward by Mr Colborne to receive the congratulations of the audience.

The only absolute novelty of importance

Press opinion afterwards was also favourable, from damning with faint praise: 'The first evening concert in the Shire Hall was in some respect the most interesting of the festival as it included the only absolute novelty of importance.' (*The Athenaeum*) This was probably written by Ebenezer Prout – Ebenezer Prout was then just about the most influential music critic of the day. The critic in *Society* magazine wrote: 'Had it not been for Mrs Meadows White's setting of the *Ode to the Passions* the Hereford Festival would hardly be worth writing about'.

Francis Hueffer in *The Times* commented that:

> Mrs Meadows is one of the few female composers of this and other countries who attempt the larger forms of orchestral music and on that count alone deserves every encouragement. Her present choice of Collins' *Ode* although intended by the poet for music does not appear at first sight a happy one, its stilted eighteenth-century diction – be it said with due reverence for the memory of the unfortunate and gifted poet does not

lend itself to musical declamation of the modern type and in spite of its title there is more reflection than passion in the pieces. But in spite of these drawbacks Mrs Meadows White has succeeded in giving charm and variety to her theme ...

Rosalind Ellicott: *not an amateur composer*

Whether it was directly connected with Alice Mary Smith's appearance can never now be known, but Rosalind Ellicott also sang one of her recently composed songs at the 1882 Festival.

At this time, Ellicott's father was the bishop of Gloucester and Bristol, but at the time of her birth in 1857 he was a professor of divinity at King's College, London and later Cambridge. He was appointed to Gloucester in 1863. Ellicott's mother, Constantia Annie, was, unlike her husband, an enthusiastic and talented amateur musician. She was a founder of the Gloucestershire Philharmonic Society, a patron of the original, nineteenth-century Cheltenham Music Festival and, in the 1880s, her musical activities in London included establishing the Handel Society Choir, hosting the Popular Ballad Concert Committee and giving prizes at the Royal Academy of Music.

Rosalind showed an aptitude for music from an early age, and in her own words 'used to run to the piano when I was only a little thing of six and play tunes to my own harmonies'. Her first music teacher was her mother, and then from the age of 12 she also took lessons from S.S. Wesley. She began composing songs from the age of 13 and, when she was 16, she entered the Royal Academy of Music as a pianist on the recommendation of William Sterndale Bennett who, as seen above, had also played a major part in Alice Mary Smith's career. Soon after this she discovered she had 'a voice' and started appearing as a soloist.

The song she sang at the 1882 Hereford Festival was one of her first in print. She had two similar songs, to words by Heine, published in 1881, with both German and English words. They are both simple Lied-like songs, which an expert has criticised as having slightly awkward vocal lines but interesting formal structures.

Probably as a result of her success, she was invited to bring a new work to the 1883 Festival in Gloucester, and the result was the song *To the Immortals*, sung and encored by Hilda Watson. She continued to compose for various musical forces, including being commissioned by Novellos the publishers for a series of violin compositions, citing Wagner as a big influence on her style. Then in 1886 she had several important performances of her work. The most prestigious of these was the premiere of her *Dramatic Overture* at the Three Choirs Festival in Gloucester. As her mother wrote to A.M. Broadley just before the Festival:

> Perhaps you are not aware that I have an artist in my own daughter. She is bringing out an Overture (her second orchestral work) at the Tuesday evening concert and to judge from its reception by the band at the rehearsal on Wednesday morning I think it is likely to produce a sensation. She calls it 'dramatic' because one of its leading features are recits for celli – I hope you will be able to hear the work on Tuesday evening. My daughter was a student at the RAM and is in all respects a member of the musical profession and *not an amateur*. You may be amused by my emphatic underlining but she is always annoyed at being spoken of as a 'talented amateur'.

The *Dramatic Overture* was indeed well received, and was praised in *The Musical Times* as a work of exceptional merit. Her other compositions for the Three Choirs, all performed at Gloucester, included *Elysium* for soprano, chorus and orchestra in 1889, which was also heard at the Cheltenham Festival that year; *Birth of Song* in 1892; *Fantasia* in A minor for piano and orchestra in 1895 (Sybil Palliser was the soloist); and in 1898 a choral ballad for male voices, *Henry of Navarre*. She was particularly proud of *Elysium*. She bought herself a brooch, using part of the cheque she had received from Novellos for it, in the form of an arrow, the feathers in diamonds, and the word 'Elysium' in pearls across it.

Rosalind was invited by the Gloucester organist, Herbert Brewer, to bring a new work to the 1898 Festival, as referred to later in Chapter 5, but turned down the opportunity, and offered the existing *Henry of Navarre* instead. In an interview published in 1891 she claimed to be able to:

> compose five different compositions in my head at the same time as I lie in bed, if I only had five pairs of hands to play them. It comes to me naturally,

I suppose, and I can assure you it is grandly exciting ... I like composing for the violin best I think. I never, however, work at night or for more than three hours at a time. I compose rapidly, and I get a whole movement in my head before I touch paper. I hardly ever alter my compositions.

It undoubtedly helped her that her father was such a well-known local figure. Yet, although most contemporary reviews of her work at the Gloucester Festivals mention him, none suggest that she obtained the opportunities because of him.

The fate of the *Ode* and Alice Mary Smith

Three further performances were given of the *Ode* in 1883. The first – by Bradford Festival Choral Society in St George's Hall, Bradford in April – was conducted by the society's director Robert Senior Burton. The second, and the one which attracted the most attention, was in a concert organised by Mrs Emma Lambourn Cock, a piano teacher and wife of a London music publisher. It was held on Monday 30 April 1883 in St James Hall, London, and was conducted by Sir William Cusins, Master of the Queen's Music, with the orchestra of the Philharmonic Society – and, by contemporary accounts, an ill-rehearsed scratch choir. The third performance of 1883 was given on the outskirts of London in December with the other main work being Sterndale Bennett's *The May Queen*. Ebenezer Prout tried to get his committee to agree to it being performed during the 1884 season of the Hackney Choral Association, but failed. The work subsequently fell out of favour and probably had only two further performances: Oxford in June 1890, and Melbourne, Australia in 1896.

Female composers at the Festival

The next female composer to appear on a Three Choirs programme was Dame Ethel Smyth. Her *Quartet in E minor* was included in the 1921 (Hereford) Festival, in a concert that also included Elgar's *Piano Quintet in A minor,* though she was not there in person. However, she was invited to be present at the 1925 Gloucester Festival to direct the *Kyrie* and *Gloria* from her *Mass in D*, and also the overture to *The Wreckers* at a secular concert. At the latter, she was said to have won enthusiastic applause from

Dame Ethel Smyth (1858–1944) was an English composer and a member of the
women's suffrage movement. Her compositions include songs, works for
piano, chamber music, orchestral works, choral works and operas
(photograph Bassano Ltd © National Portrait Gallery, London)

the audience. The Gloucester organist, Sir Herbert Brewer, proudly noted
later that this was 'the first occasion on which a woman composer had
been seen or heard as a conductor in a cathedral'. Brewer was a big supporter of Smyth and wrote to *The Morning Post* on her behalf after the
1925 Festival, in a piece that was republished by the *Gloucester Journal*.
Under a heading of 'Dr. Brewer on a neglected composer', he wrote:

> ... it was my privilege to introduce an incomprehensibly neglected choral
> composer, Dame Ethel Smyth. Speaking as one who knows his public, I

have no hesitation in saying that whether one judges by the feeling in the Cathedral at the time or by subsequent comments heard on all sides, the two numbers from her *Mass in D* made a profound impression. How the music gripped the chorus and all concerned in the production could, I think, be felt in their rendering of it; in short, the work under the composer's baton was a most impressive and inspired performance, and I have had many requests ... to perform the Mass in its entirety in the near future.

Dame Ethel Smyth was invited back by Brewer to conduct the whole of her *Mass in D* at the 1928 Gloucester Festival but he unfortunately did not live to see it. Required by the dean to cover her head while conducting in the cathedral, Dame Ethel apparently wore her doctoral cap and gown but quickly found the cap to be an irritating encumbrance which she discarded with a jerk of the head – legend has it that it landed either on the desk of the leader of the orchestra, Billy Reed, or in the dean's lap!

She had written to Brewer's successor, Herbert Sumsion, in June 1928:

I fancy that by now you will have taken over the rather heavy legacy dear Sir Herbert left you. This is just to say that I am here [Bath] till the 21st June; that to come over and rehearse from here is a light matter, as regards time & money, compared to coming all the way from Woking – that if you could possibly fit in a rehearsal of the Mass for me before I go ... the end of this week would be an ideal time – I shld be very glad indeed.

It is not known whether this request was granted.

Following this, the Worcester Festival of 1969 witnessed the premiere of Elizabeth Maconchy's *And death shall have no more dominion*. But a further 24 years had to pass before the next premiere by a female composer. This was Diana Burrell's *Veni creator* at the 1993 Worcester Festival. However, since then, many women composers have seen first performances of their work at Three Choirs Festivals. These include Eleanor Alberga, Sally Beamish, Judith Bingham, Kerensa Briggs, Emily Doolittle, Shiva Feshareki, Nilufar Habibian, Charlotte Harding, Cheryl Frances-Hoad, Dani Howard, Eleanor Kercher, Liz Lane, Sally Lamb McCune, Olivia Sparkhall, Dobrinka Tabakova, Hilary Tann and Jennifer Watson.

Edward Elgar

Public Hall, Worcester: 9 September 1890

On Wednesday evening 9 September 1890, in the Public Hall, Worcester, in front of an audience of 793, Edward Elgar took the podium for the first time at a Three Choirs concert to conduct the premiere of his Froissart Overture.

B Y THIS TIME, the Festival repertoire was expanding and, as well as the now-established continental composers such as Spohr, Mendelssohn and Rossini, it included contemporary ones such as Brahms, Gounod, Dvořák, Wagner and Verdi. Mendelssohn was the favourite of the late Victorians, and his *Elijah* was a fixture at the Three Choirs. The choral music of J.S. Bach was also starting to be regularly programmed. These all took their positions alongside long-term favourites such as Mozart's *Requiem* and Haydn's *Creation*. And *Messiah,* obviously. Beethoven's *Mass in C* and *Mount of Olives* had been popular mid-century, but had fallen out of favour by 1890.

In addition, there was also a greater focus on introducing the works of contemporary British composers and, if possible, securing a premiere conducted by them. Parry, Sullivan, Barnby, Stainer and Mackenzie came under this category, and each centre would vie with the others as to who could produce the best 'novelties', as these were known.

Sir Edward Elgar (1857–1934) was first approached by the Festival committee for a new short orchestral work in November 1889. The resulting piece – his *Froissart Overture* – was premiered in the Public Hall, Worcester at the 1890 Festival. The first of a long and successful partnership with the Three Choirs

Local music teacher and jobbing composer

Known at this time as a local music teacher, member of the Festival orchestra and jobbing composer, Elgar was approached by the Festival committee for a new short orchestral work in November 1889. The commission had come at an opportune moment. At that time, Elgar was singularly failing to set the London music world alight and despairing of receiving any recognition or encouragement. Correspondence exists between the Worcester organist, William Done, and Elgar, with Elgar sending Done a copy of his newly published *Salut d'Amour*. On 1 January 1890, Done wrote to Elgar:

> Thank you very much for your kind letters and for your good wishes of the Season. I shall be pleased to receive the score of your new composition (it will probably come tomorrow) and I shall study it with much pleasure as the work of one whose talent I have always recognised and admired. It will be a pleasure to you to know that the proposal to introduce your orchestral piece at the Festival met with no opposition. I must not take the credit of it to myself, as it scarcely required a word of recommendation from me. I will take care to give you a good orchestra and fair opportunity of rehearsal. Will you kindly tell me whether any extra instruments will be required. I hope not as the orchestra is so small.

This implies that the decision to commission had been Done's own, and it had been sanctioned by the Festival committee. The committee may have been encouraged to give their approval by the fact that, through marrying Alice Roberts the year before, Elgar had married into the Worcester 'county' set. There could also have been some promptings from the young Worcester assistant organist and friend of Elgar, Hugh Blair.

On 4 January Done wrote again:

> The score of your little work arrived safely. Many thanks to you for it. At the last Festival we had both Tuba and Contra Fag, but I don't intend to go to the expense of both this time. I myself much prefer the Contra Fag. One of the two we must have, but as Mr Williams will conduct throughout the Festival I must leave him to decide which and will let you know as soon as I hear from him.

Elgar composed *Froissart* between April and July 1890. Jean Froissart, a French romantic chronicler of the fourteenth century, was the inspiration behind it, and it is believed Elgar adopted the title from Sir Walter Scott's poem *Old Mortality* in which the heroic figure John Graham quotes from Froissart to incite chivalry among his followers. At nearly 15 minutes long when completed, it was Elgar's longest orchestral movement to date.

On 29 July he wrote to a friend that:

> My overture is finished & do not think will be liked but that must take
> its chance: I find in my limited experience that one's own friends are the
> people to be most in dread of: I could fill a not unentertaining book with
> the criticisms passed on my former efforts ...

In June and July, he offered the score to the publishers Novello's and Goodwin *&* Tabb.

And then on 2 July 1890, Done wrote:

> Mr Wheeler [Hon. Sec., Worcester Musical Festival] has forwarded me
> your note. I will take care to have your piece properly inserted in the
> programme. The London rehearsals will take place at St George's Hall
> on Wednesday and Thursday, September 3rd and 4th. Our conductor
> has sent me a rehearsal programme, and I find that he has put you down
> for 3 o'clock on the first day – <u>Wednesday 3rd</u>. I hope to hear that that
> arrangement will suit you. You shall have a programme as soon as they are
> ready. I hope you are well.

On 31 July, Elgar heard from Novello's that they were unlikely to publish *Froissart* 'because there is so little demand for that class of music'. However, they subsequently had a change of heart, and on 8 August he heard that they had after all accepted it for publication.

A minor premiere

Prior to the Festival, probably the most anticipated premiere was Bridge's *Repentance of Ninevah* in the Thursday morning concert. At this time, Frederick Bridge was organist of Westminster Abbey and a tutor at the Royal

Portrait of Edward Elgar by Charles Frederick Grindrod, 1903
(© National Portrait Gallery, London)

College of Music. Composing was a spare-time activity, but an important one for him, although he was never considered a major talent. Described as a dramatic oratorio, with text by Joseph Bennett and conducted by the composer, the *Annals* reported that Bridge 'had every reason to be satisfied with the performance, at that time adjudged to be his greatest'. He had the top soloists alongside him, among them Emma Albani, Hilda Wilson and Edward Lloyd. The chorus – which that year was drawn from Cardiff, and 80 gentlemen and ladies from Leeds, as well as the three cities – and band apparently 'acquitted themselves admirably', though the 'invisible choir', who were placed beneath the orchestra and 'so sang under difficulties', became 'painfully flat'. Bridge notes with pride this piece in his memoirs, and reported that Madame Albani later sang from it to the Queen at Balmoral. And he obviously impressed the Festival because he subsequently had three more premieres – 1892, 1894 and 1901. The morning concert concluded with Beethoven's *Engendi*.

Other Festival premieres included Hugh Blair's *Jubilate in D*, and *To morning*, a part-song by C.H. Lloyd.

Due to the elderly Done also being ill, the Festival conductor-in-chief was Charles Lee Williams, the Gloucester organist. The rest of the programme, as planned by Done, included Mendelssohn's *St Paul* and *Elijah*, Beethoven's *Engendi* and *Symphony in C minor*, Spohr's *God thou art great*, Haydn's *Creation* (parts one and two), Mozart's *Requiem* and, of local interest, Lee Williams' *Bethany*. In the concerts of miscellaneous music, the diet included: Bach, represented by the cantata (sung in English in those days) *A stronghold sure* and the *pastoral symphony* from the *Christmas Oratorio*; Weber's *Jubilee Cantata*; Parry's *Ode on St Cecilia's Day*; Greig's *Peer Gynt*; and the introduction to the third part of Wagner's *Lohengrin*.

As ever, the week concluded with a performance of *Messiah*.

A very favourable impression

Elgar's composing and conducting debut in all this was scheduled for the Wednesday evening secular concert, held in Worcester's Public Hall, with its notoriously unsympathetic acoustics. It was a sell-out, with 'scarcely a seat being left vacant' according to *The Musical Times*. The *Annals* describes the occasion as: 'A new overture *Froissart*, composed and conducted by Mr Edward Elgar, was included in the programme and created a very favourable impression,' having described all the other items:

> In the evening, when the only miscellaneous secular selection of music
> was given, Dr Parry's *Ode to St Cecilia's Day*, written for the Leeds Festival
> shortly before, was performed. The composer conducted, and the beauties

of this admirable work were displayed, the solos being sung by Miss Anna Williams and Mr Watkin-Mills. The choir, later in the programme, gave a fine rendering of Dr C. Harford Lloyd's part song *To Morning,* for eight-part chorus unaccompanied, composed especially for this Festival. The solos included Beethoven's *Ah Perfido,* sung by Mrs Hutchinson; a scene from *La Juive* by Mr Edward Lloyd; a duett [sic] from Gounod's *Romeo et Juliette,* for two singers just named; an Irish ditty and a German song by Mr Plunket Greene. The suite for orchestra, *Peer Gynt* by Grieg, was well played, and the introduction to the third act of *Lohengrin* carefully performed.

Mr Elgar will do good work

The reviews in the press were generally favourable, most suggesting that Elgar was a composer to watch for the future, with some reservations on the musical content. Joseph Bennett in *The Daily Telegraph* felt that 'Mr Elgar has ideas and feeling as well as aspiration, and should be encouraged to persevere. He will one day arrive'. This opinion wasn't entirely unexpected given that Elgar had courted Bennett by letter in 1889, and he proved to be a powerful ally in the press. Elgar's characteristic opinion was that it was 'much liked by the *musicians* present'. *The Musical Times* reported it as:

> a romantic Concert-Overture, entitled 'Froissart'. Mr Elgar, formerly
> of Worcester, is now, we believe, a resident in London, where, it may
> be hoped, and given opportunity, even expected that he will make
> his mark. The Overture is of course chivalric in style, and, perhaps,
> more commendable for what it tries to say than for the manner of its
> expression. There is upon it, what surprises no one – the mark of youth
> and inexperience; but it shows that, with further thought and study, Mr
> Elgar will do good work. He must acquire greater coherence of ideas, and
> conciseness of utterance – those inevitable signs of a master, only to be
> attained by extended and arduous effort. For such effort, no doubt, Mr
> Elgar may be trusted. 'Froissart' was much applauded – the Prophet had
> honour even in his own country.

The *Manchester Guardian* referenced its 'spirited themes' but also 'excessive elaboration and tendency to monotony'.

Despite the poor acoustic of the public hall, Elgar was pleased by the way the work was received. He wrote to his friend Frank Webb on 28 September, 'I have had very good notices in nearly all the papers especially in those most to be feared ...'.

Elgar and the Festival

In the audience was the Hereford assistant organist, Ivor Atkins, who was overwhelmed by the music and its composer. It was to be the start of a life-long friendship between the two men.

Froissart was performed again in Birmingham in February 1891; however, it had to wait another ten years to be heard in London, even though Elgar had taken the parts to August Manns to try and get it played on one of his Crystal Palace programmes. It was therefore not generally taken up by conductors. However, the composer himself still rated it. As he said nine years after composing it, 'it's old and not quite what I would write now, but it's good healthy stuff'. After it, Elgar moved back to choral music and returned to his *Black Knight* sketches.

An enhanced reputation

No works by Elgar were programmed by the Three Choirs Festival for another six years. In the meantime, his reputation was enhanced by the success of his cantata *The Black Knight* and several part songs. By now he was also making an annual pilgrimage to Wagner's Bayreuth Festival; but in 1893 he was reminded of reality by being engaged to play in that year's Festival orchestra. Among the pieces he played for was Parry's recently-composed oratorio, *Job*. Elgar was deeply impressed by it: 'I played first violin because of the fee as I cd. not get recognition as a composer'. In fact, this was to be his last Festival as a member of the orchestra. The tide began to turn in 1896 when his *Lux Christi (Light of Life)* was premiered at the Worcester Festival of 1896. Like the *Black Knight*, the oratorio owed its existence to the friendship Elgar had with Hugh Blair. And then the Hereford Festival of 1897 saw the premiere of his *Te Deum and Benedictus*, dedicated to Sinclair. However, after then, no major work by Elgar had a Three Choirs first performance. This was not for want of trying by the cathedral organists. But Elgar, always short of money, could never overlook that Three Choirs commissions

Rehearsal of the Three Choirs chorus at Hereford, 1900 (© Hereford Cathedral)

were honorary, whereas the Leeds and Birmingham Festivals paid. It was also because he was busy with *Caractacus* that Elgar refused Brewer's request for a new work for Gloucester in 1898 (Brewer having already been turned down by Rosalind Ellicott), and urged him to apply to Coleridge-Taylor with the result that *Ballade in A minor* was first performed. However, his generosity to colleagues whom he liked is also illustrated by his orchestrating Blair's *Advent Cantata* in 1894 and Brewer's *Emmaus* in 1901.

Elgar approached Atkins for a symphony for Worcester in 1899 (Atkins' first Festival) as no one had commissioned him for the major orchestral work he wanted to compose. He suggested the theme of General Gordon, who was at that time a national hero, but the lack of money meant it was never likely to happen. At this time, Elgar was working on the *Enigma Variations*, which had their first performance under Richter in 1899. This work established Elgar as the leading English composer of the day, and set him on course for a European reputation. Atkins seized the first available opportunity to introduce the work to the Festival three months later. This was its third performance, but the first to be conducted by Elgar, and the first in the form the work is known today, with the revised and expanded finale. However, like *Froissart,* the work was performed in the dreadful acoustics of Worcester's Public Hall.

European recognition

In 1900 at Hereford, the only Elgar performed was a scene from *Caractacus,* and in 1901 Elgar conducted his new *Cockaigne* overture and the *Prelude and Angel's Farewell* from *Gerontius*. Atkins again tried to get a new work for 1902 but Elgar recommended Walford Davies and Horatio Parker, and asked that *The Dream of Gerontius* be performed in full. He did however contribute arrangements for brass of chorales from Bach's *St Matthew Passion*, which were performed from the top of the cathedral tower, partly to celebrate the publication that year of his and Atkins' edition of that work. In the meantime, *Gerontius* had been produced at the Birmingham Festival of 1900 and had received an inadequate performance. But by 1902, Elgar had heard two magnificent performances in Düsseldorf and knew that his original vision could be realised. The Worcester Festival performance was the first professional performance to be conducted by the composer. Not quite in the original version or complete. It was 'Protestantised' to make it 'appropriate' for a performance in an Anglican cathedral, but Elgar didn't mind that; he just wanted a decent performance of the music for the first time in England, and for the first time in the cathedral acoustic for which it was designed. *Gerontius* went on to be performed at 18 more Three Choirs during his lifetime, all but four being conducted by himself. That historic performance at Worcester marked the end of the beginning of Elgar's relationship with the Festivals. Thereafter, he was no longer the local man who needed help to make good. By 1904, when he conducted *The Apostles* at Gloucester, he was Sir Edward, friend of the king, and soon-to-be an honorary freeman of the City of Worcester.

He now took houses for the Festival weeks and entertained with flair and zest. Into the Festivals now came his friends, the wealthy connoisseur Frank Schuster, the MP's wife and Millais' daughter, Alice Stuart-Wortley, and the rich American Mrs Julia Worthington.

Up to and including 1913, the last of the pre-war Festivals, *The Apostles* was performed in 1904, 1905, 1906, 1907 and 1909; *The Kingdom* in 1907 and 1908; *Cockaigne* in 1901, 1902 and 1909; *In the South* in 1904; the *Introduction and Allegro for Strings* in 1905 and 1906; the *Coronation March* in 1911; the *first symphony* in 1909 and 1910; the *second symphony* in 1911 and 1913, and the *Violin Concerto* in 1911. Nearly all these performances were

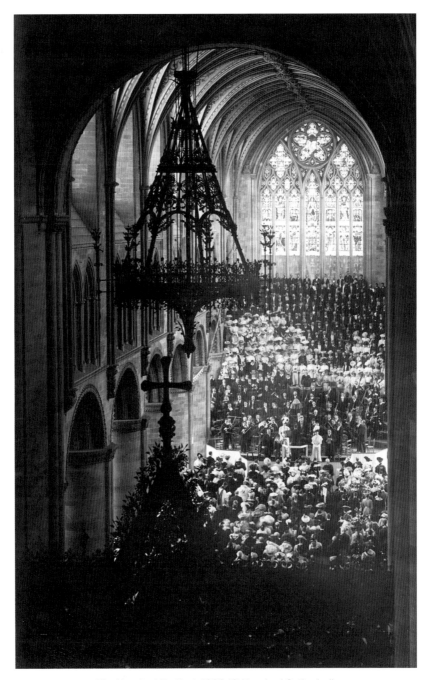

The Hereford Festival, 1906 (© Hereford Cathedral)

conducted by Elgar himself. Three first performances were given in this period, the choral song *Go song of mine* (Hereford 1909), the *Wand of Youth Suite no.2* at Worcester in 1908 and the *Suite from the Crown of India* at Hereford in 1912. Yet the most important 'first performance' was that at Gloucester in 1910 as discussed in Chapter 7, the *Violin Concerto*.

No one wants my music

In the immediate post-war Festivals, Elgar cut a sad and lonely figure. His wife was dead, Parry and Sinclair were also gone. And millions had been killed in action. He conducted his *For the fallen, The Dream of Gerontius*, the *Introduction and Allegro* and the *Music Makers* at Worcester in 1920. He went on to conduct the latter three times at the post-war Festivals. As well as feeling personally lonely, he was also convinced that 'no one wants my music' and that music in England was 'dying fast'. However, in these years he still looked to help the young. He welcomed Percy Hull taking over from Sinclair at Hereford, and recommended Holst's *Hymn of Jesus* to him. It subsequently appeared at the 1921 Festival. And to Brewer, he suggested commissioning Eugene Goossens, Herbert Howells and Arthur

Commercial Road, Hereford, decorated during the 1906 Festival
(courtesy of Derek Foxton)

Bliss to compose new works for the 1922 Festival. This did not mean that he liked the music of the younger composers. He is known not to have liked the *Hymn of Jesus* or appreciated the finer points of Bliss's *Colour Symphony*, which led to a several-year fracture in his friendship with Bliss. And according to William Walton's wife and biographer, he had sharp words to say to Walton about his *Viola Concerto* when the composer conducted it at the 1932 Worcester Festival with Lionel Tertis as the soloist:

> William met Elgar in the lavatory. He didn't much care for William's work, and was heard to mutter that William had murdered the poor unfortunate instrument. The great man was only interested in hearing from William what the horse racing results were.

He also continued to be sensitive to what he imagined would be other composers' attitudes to his works. He is reported to have snapped at Vaughan Williams at the rehearsal of the *Cello Concerto*, 'I'm surprised you come to hear this vulgar music'.

Elgar and Beatrice Harrison rehearsing the *Cello Concerto* at the end of 1919
(© Elgar Birthplace Museum)

Uncrowned Three Choirs monarch

In 1923, Elgar left London and returned to live in Worcestershire, when the third stage of his relationship with the Three Choirs Festival began: that of being their uncrowned monarch. His fame, residing in the district and his undoubted superiority as a conductor of his own music, now lent the Festival the special aura of being in partnership with one of the great musical figures of the time. In a unique way, they became Elgar festivals. Elgar was also the intermediary between the Gramophone Company and the Festival that ultimately led to the recording of the 1927 Hereford Festival, for which he composed a *Civic Fanfare* – and also one of the reasons why some of the discs survived to be issued despite not being up to the Company's standard. As one of their recording artists, the company first approached Elgar prior to the 1926 Worcester Festival for him to liaise with the Festival and cathedral for the recordings to be made of that event, but that did not work out. Elgar also tried to perform a similar function for the 1928 Gloucester Festival, but again the local dean and chapter were against any recording being made.

The Gramophone Company (HMV) mobile recording van outside Hereford Cathedral while making the first ever recording of the Festival, in 1927. The concert featured the Festival chorus with the London Symphony Orchestra and soloists Horace Stevens, Margaret Balfour and Tudor Davies, conducted (with the exception of the Brewer item) by Sir Edward Elgar (courtesy of Derek Foxton)

But there was no new music from him. 'New' works appeared but they were reworkings of material composed years before. According to Wulstan Atkins, he did consider composing a new work for the 1929 Worcester Festival, a setting of two poems by Shelley, *The Demon* and *Adonais*, but this was vetoed by the dean on the grounds that *Adonais* 'is frankly pagan'.

From 1920 to 1934, when he died, Elgar was, according to his biographer, Michael Kennedy, that saddest of spectacles, a composer who – to use his own phrase – had 'gone out'. He did not look sad though. In the cathedrals, he conducted in court dress or in the robes of one of his doctorates. At his own house parties, he was immaculately dressed, often in a white summer suit. He was portly now, his hair white, his moustache luxuriant. He carried a stick as he grew older. He could be seen talking to his close friends: Percy Hull, Billy Reed, Herbert Brewer, Ivor Atkins and, after Brewer died, Herbert Sumsion. The great friend of his last years, George Bernard Shaw, was a regular Festival visitor, as was Worcestershire-born, former Prime Minister, Stanley Baldwin. Over time, he grew to enjoy Vaughan Williams' company and to appreciate works like Vaughan Williams' *Sancta Civitas*. However, he is said to have often left a rehearsal in the cathedral to go to the Hereford Club to discover who won the 3.30, telling people there he knew nothing about music and had no interest in it.

Hereford 1933 was to be his last Festival. During it, he conducted *The Kingdom*, *The Dream of Gerontius* and the *Cello Concerto* in its viola version. Billy Reed found him more than usually tired, but he had taken a house for the week and sat in the garden speaking to his friends and anyone who dropped in for tea, and gave George Bernard Shaw lessons in the finer points of Mendelssohn's orchestration in *Elijah*. However, what was thought to be sciatica turned out to be a malignant tumour pressing on his sciatic nerve, and five months later he died.

Since 1934 ....

Through the ongoing presence of the cathedral organists who had worked with him, there was a living Festival link with Elgar until Sumsion retired in 1967. In the immediate aftermath of his death, it was agreed that the conducting of his works should be shared among the three organists. This sharing not only released the host from the responsibility of taking over the huge burden

Edward Elgar conducting. Photograph by Herbert Lambert, for Elliott & Fry, 1942
(© National Portrait Gallery, London)

of conducting that was created by Elgar's absence, but it was also the incentive for establishing a pattern of conducting responsibilities which still holds to this day. The Festival following his death was reportedly, and understandably, full of extraordinary feelings of emotion and grief for the participants. A feeling of sadness dominated the whole week, and it became extremely difficult to develop any sort of Festival atmosphere. In the following year, after an emotional performance of *The Dream of Gerontius*, the Elgar memorial window was unveiled in Worcester Cathedral. It is in the north aisle, above his favourite spot for listening to so many performances of his works.

Festival conductors have come and gone since 1934, but Elgar's music continues to feature prominently in the programmes. It is still true to say, as Samuel Langford wrote in the *Manchester Guardian* in 1924:

It is hardly too much to say that he who has not heard Elgar's music at
these Festivals only half knows what Elgar is. Elgar is a romantic spirit,
the roots of whose being are in the past, in a way that cannot be felt
everywhere as it is here. Worcester, the faithful city, is faithful enough
to the association in which it is born to give it a setting that takes the
imagination back far enough to feel whence strength has come. The very

Famous living British composers as featured in *The Illustrated London News*, October
1908. Pictured are: Mr Granville Bantock, Mr Josif Holbrooke, Mr Coleridge-Taylor,
Mr Percy Pitt, Mr Cyril Scott, Mr Hamilton Harty, Sir George Clement Martin, Miss Ethel
Smyth, Dr Ebenezer Prout, Dr Henry Walford Davies, Dr William Hayman Cummings,
Mr Edward German, Sir Walter Parratt, Sir Charles Villiers Stanford, Sir Edward Elgar,
Dr Frederic Hymen Cowen, Sir Alexander Campbell Mackenzie, Sir Hubert Hastings
Parry and Sir Frederick Bridge (© National Portrait Gallery, London)

walls cry out to us from the same romantic past that has bred his music. His music, heard within them, is redolent of England in the complete sense which in other places may fail it. (Samuel Langford writing in the *Manchester Guardian* in 1924)

FROM TOP LEFT: Sir Ivor Atkins, Percy Hull, Herbert Sumsion and Edward Elgar (seated), Hereford, 1921 (courtesy of Derek Foxton)

6

Ralph Vaughan Williams

Gloucester Cathedral: 6 September 1910

On Tuesday 6 September 1910 the audience in Gloucester Cathedral witnessed the premiere of Vaughan Williams' Fantasia on a Theme by Thomas Tallis.

B Y THIS TIME, younger men had taken the Festival into the new century, and the three cathedral organists – Ivor Atkins, Herbert Brewer
and George Robertson Sinclair – were growing in confidence, raising standards and widening the repertoire. The Festival itself had settled into a pattern of a festal service led by the chorus and orchestra at the beginning of
the week, on the Sunday afternoon. That service still included the 'charity'
sermon preached by an eminent divine. There were 'oratorio' performances
in the cathedral on four days and two evenings, and the festival closed with
a performance of Handel's *Messiah*. In addition, there was a single secular
concert (and sometimes a chamber concert), and liturgical week-day services
were sung by the resident cathedral choir, augmented by representatives
from the other two cathedral choirs.

In the repertory, Bach was now well-established, Verdi and Wagner had
made their first appearances. And of the native composers, Elgar had joined
Parry in having a secure foothold on the programmes. Two new names made
their first appearances in the early years of the century: Granville Bantock
and Walford Davies. The Festival directors continued to look to commission
new works – 'novelties', as Brewer later explained when looking back over
the discussions he had while planning his first Festival in 1898: 'I pointed
out that if musical interest was not maintained, and if the programmes

Ralph Vaughan Williams (1872–1958) by Walter Stoneman, 1936
(© National Portrait Gallery, London)

contained no novelties, the Festivals would soon cease to attract, and would pass away like other worn-out institutions'.

A timeless vision

It was in this spirit that Herbert Brewer approached the young composer Ralph Vaughan Williams in 1910 for a new short orchestral piece to be programmed in the same concert as Elgar was to conduct the first complete performance in Gloucester Cathedral of his recent success, *The Dream of Gerontius*. Vaughan Williams accepted and drew upon his knowledge of Gloucester Cathedral's ambiance and acoustics, his growing interest in Tudor music and his editorial role on the recently-published English Hymnal to produce the now-iconic *Fantasia on a Theme by Thomas Tallis*. According to his widow, Ursula, he had:

> chosen his forces with the Norman architecture in mind; the solo quartet and first and second group of strings make dramatic use of the resonance of the stone, in their answer and echo in his use of the music Tallis wrote for Archbishop Parker's *Psalter* of 1567.

The Tallis *Fantasia* is set for a string quartet and double string orchestra and has a grave beauty, and although only 20 minutes in length, its string spread chords give it power, massive spaciousness and a four-square solidity. As *The Times'* reviewer soon after the first performance wrote, 'It cannot be assigned to a time or school but it is full of the visions which have haunted the seers of all times'.

By that time, although Vaughan Williams was not exactly a household name, he had already had orchestral and choral works performed by Dan Godfrey and Henry Wood, both conductors who encouraged British composers and were prepared to include new works in their programmes. He was also regularly giving lectures and writing articles for musical journals and for the second edition of *Grove's Dictionary of Music and Musicians* (1904–10), as well as his aforementioned editorship of the *English Hymnal*. He had also already composed and published well-regarded music, such as the songs, *Linden Lea* (1902) and *Silent Noon* (1904), the tone poem *In the Fen Country* (1904–07), the song cycle *Songs of Travel* (1905) and the *Norfolk*

Gloucester Cathedral during an Edwardian Civic Service

Rhapsody No.1 (1906). Brewer has left no details, but there is little doubt that he was well aware of Vaughan Williams at the time of this commissioning.

A distinguished gathering

The programme Brewer put together for the 1910 Festival included what had become standard fare in terms of music and scheduling in the early years of the twentieth century, and Vaughan Williams was only one of the composers invited to bring new works. Others included Granville Bantock, Basil Harwood, Charles Lee Williams and Brewer himself.

As usual also, there was a distinguished gathering of guest performers. These included the singers Agnes Nicholls, Clementine De Vere Sapio, Amy Simpson, Cicely Gleeson-White, Ada Crossley, Edith Clegg, Mildred Jones, Phyllis Lett, John Coates, Plunket Greene, Frederic Austin, William Higley and Robert Radford. Solo violinists included Fritz Kreisler and Muriel Pickup. The now celebrated W.H. (Billy) Reed led the orchestra, mostly by now made up of members of the London Symphony Orchestra, for the first of many occasions. Also, a recent innovation was the engagement of instrumental soloists to play in the cathedral. Up to a few years earlier they were only employed for the secular concerts.

After an organ recital of music by S.S. Wesley, the opening service began with a performance of Sullivan's *In Memorium* in memory of the late king, Edward VII, who had died a few months earlier. The service also included a *Magnificat and Nunc Dimittis* composed by Ivor Atkins, the last movement of Brahms' *Symphony in C minor* and Handel's *Largo in C* with Muriel Pickup on the violin.

In the Wednesday morning concert, on the day following Vaughan Williams' debut, there were what the *Annals* describes as 'two modern works of much interest'. These were Parry's motet *Beyond these voices*, followed by Elgar's *A flat symphony*, each conducted by their respective composers. After the interval there was the much-anticipated new Basil Harwood *Organ Concerto*. And after this came the unaccompanied motet by Lee Williams, *The Lord's Prayer*. The programme ended with Goetz's cantata *By the waters of Babylon*.

During the Wednesday evening concert, Parry was invited to receive the thanks of the mayor of Gloucester for his part in securing an extension to the Shire Hall concert hall. On the programme was Parry's *Ode to music* and Brewer's suite for orchestra and chorus, *Summer Sports*. Also performed was the Stanford song cycle *Cushendall* and violin solos by Kreisler.

On Thursday morning, there was, according to the *Annals*, an 'atmosphere of modernity' as Brewer conducted Richard Strauss's *Tod und Verklarung*, followed by Verdi's *Requiem*. After the interval, Beethoven's *Eroica* was followed by Lloyd's motet *The righteous live for evermore*.

Thursday evening witnessed Bantock conducting his own oratorio, *Gethsemane*, followed by a Bach violin concerto played by Kreisler (incidentally, the first instrumental piece by Bach programmed at a Three Choirs Festival). At the end, Kreisler bowed low and gracefully to the audience – also the first time this had been done by any performer in the Festival's history. The concert finished with Mendelssohn's *Hymn of Praise*. And on the final day there was the traditional performance of *Messiah*.

An inauspicious debut

Sandwiched into this august programme, the concert on Tuesday 6 September was remarkable only for being devoted to the first complete performance in Gloucester, albeit suitably Protestantised, of Elgar's *The Dream of Gerontius*, with full orchestra and chorus of 260. According to much contemporary opinion, the premiere of Ralph Vaughan Williams' new work was a mere footnote.

That is certainly how it appeared to the over 2,000 audience members in Gloucester Cathedral. The only comment by the *Annals* on the other item on the programme was 'Dr Vaughan Williams also conducted a new work'. Neither was it considered the most noteworthy premiere of the Festival. That honour was shared by the new works introduced by Granville Bantock and Basil Harwood.

It was the tradition at that time in Three Choirs Festival history for composers to conduct their own works where feasible. So Vaughan Williams made his Three Choirs conducting debut in Gloucester Cathedral that September evening, in front of the packed nave which included Edward Elgar and two of Herbert Brewer's pupils, later to become famous composers themselves, Ivor Gurney and Herbert Howells. Though a local boy, born in Down Ampney in 1872, this was Vaughan Williams' first known visit to the Festival since being taken by his mother as a small child as part of his early musical education.

Contemporary opinion wasn't enthusiastic, including that of the majority of the audience according to the local paper's music critic:

> the impression left on the mind by the whole composition was of unsatisfaction ... We had short phrases repeated with tiresome literation and at no time did the *Fantasia* rise beyond the level of an uninteresting exercise ... there was a feeling of relief when [it] came to an end and we could listen to something with more colour and warmth.

The Musical Times critic described it as: '... exhibiting power and much charm of the contemplative kind, but it appeared overlong for the subject matter'.

Critical response to *Gerontius* was more predictable, with Elgar already a local favourite. The *Annals* reported that it was anticipation of that event that had filled the cathedral, which is most likely the case, and said that *Gerontius* is heard to 'best advantage' in a sacred building.

Sir Granville Bantock (1868–1946) by Herbert Lambert, 1922
(© National Portrait Gallery, London)

However, not everyone was unaware of the *Fantasia*'s significance on first hearing. Herbert Howells later recalled:

> Lovely first week of September came. With it came ... [Ralph Vaughan Williams] ... I was seeing him for the first time. But what mattered was that it was Tuesday night, an Elgar night; a dedicated Elgar audience, all devotees of the by then 'accepted' masterpiece *The Dream of Gerontius* ... But there, conducting a strange work for strings, RVW himself, a comparative (or complete?) stranger; and his Fantasy would be holding up the Dream, maybe for ten minutes? In fact, for twice ten, as it happened. He left the rostrum, in the non-applauding silence of those days, thanks be! And he came to the empty chair next to mine, carrying a copy of *Gerontius*, and presently was sharing it with me, while Elgar was conducting the first hearing I ever had of the Dream. For a music bewildered youth of seventeen it was an overwhelming evening, so disturbing and moving that I even asked RVW for his autograph – and got it.

After the performance, Howells met up with fellow pupil Ivor Gurney and they are reported to have 'wandered the streets of Gloucester for hours unwilling to return home and unable to sleep from the power of the experience they had just shared'. Howells later described the *Fantasia* as 'a supreme commentary by one great composer upon another'. And no one is likely to disagree.

'Novelties' of note

Opinion of the other works premiered at the Festival was more positive, *The Musical Times* devoting a whole separate article to a review of Basil Harwood's *Concerto for Organ and Orchestra*, describing it as 'an important work [which] deserves special notice'. Harwood was then considered a major composer, particularly for the organ, and the young Herbert Howells was around that same time using Harwood's compositions as models for his own organ sonata. The Granville Bantock work, *Gethsemane*, for soloists, chorus and orchestra, was also eagerly anticipated, the *Annals* reporting that there were 'some thrilling moments, and the masterly handling of the orchestra (by the composer) was most impressive'. *The Musical Times* was also impressed: 'Its production was looked forward to with great interest ... the music ... is constantly interesting because of its power and originality ... there are some thrilling moments, and the orchestral devices always hold the attention'. Bantock was also considered to be a major composer at that time, demonstrated by the fact that Elgar dedicated one of his *Pomp and Circumstance* marches to him, and Sibelius his *Third Symphony. Gethsemane* was an extract from a never-completed work, *Christus, a Festival Symphony* intended to be in ten parts for solo voices, chorus and orchestra.

The contributions of the local composers – Charles Lee Williams' unaccompanied motet for eight-part chorus, *The Lord's Prayer* and Brewer's suite for chorus and orchestra, *Summer Sports* – were also remarked on favourably by the *Annals*. Lee Williams had been Brewer's predecessor in the Gloucester organ loft. Both men took their composing seriously, and produced many capable works, Brewer in particular. His *Summer Sports* was programmed alongside Hubert Parry's *Ode to music* set for soloists, chorus and orchestra during a concert in the Shire Hall, and both works were, according to the

No. 9 College Green, Gloucester – scene of the first semi-public performance of Elgar's *Violin Concerto* in 1910 With Billy Reed on violin and Elgar on piano (© D. Eaketts)

Annals, 'received with enthusiasm'. Brewer's suite also impressed *The Musical Times* in its revealing of 'the fluency and inventiveness of the composer ... a good deal of the effect of the suite is to be found in the orchestral accompaniment, but the vocal writing is always interesting and melodious'. Lee Williams' motet was premiered during the same morning concert that also saw the first appearance of the Harwood, as well as a Parry motet and Elgar's first, and at that time only, symphony. For *The Musical Times* reviewer, it was 'one of the abiding recollections of the Festival'. It was repeated at two further Gloucester festivals in the 1920s, and is still in print.

There was another deeply significant first performance at the 1910 Festival, but one given to a small and private audience – Elgar's *Violin Concerto*. He had composed it during that summer and asked the leader of the Festival orchestra, Billy Reed, to play it through at the house near the cathedral where he was lodging for the week, now known as 9 College Green. Elgar was to play the orchestral parts on the piano. Reed already knew it well, having helped Elgar through the composition process.

However, the prospect still daunted him, as he later recalled:

> I knew every note of the concerto, and exactly how he liked it played ...
> yet I felt a little overwhelmed at being asked to play the solo part in what
> would actually be the first performance before an audience ... When the
> time arrived I went over to the house and found the guests assembled.
> Nearly all the prominent musicians engaged at the Festival were there ...
> [and] some music critics ... The room was full ...

The performance went well, and the *Concerto* was duly given its official premiere, with Fritz Kreisler, who had also played through it with Elgar during the week, as the soloist in London a couple of months later.

An enduring relationship

Despite the mixed initial reaction, the *Fantasia* quickly established itself in the classical repertoire. At the Three Choirs Festival alone, the work would appear under the composer's baton three more times, in 1921, 1938 and 1948. Its first London performance took place in 1913, it was broadcast by the BBC in 1926 and first recorded in 1936. Vaughan Williams had amended it in

1913, and again in 1919 prior to its publication in 1921. He cut out passages that he felt were unduly repetitious and generally tightened it up.

The 1936 recording, made by the embryonic Decca company under the supervision of Vaughan Williams, was subsequently declared by *The Gramophone* magazine to be one of the outstanding records of the year, and was reissued on the Dutton label in 1994. The conductor was Boyd Neel, himself a regular Three Choirs guest, and the orchestra his own string orchestra. Neel had been a pupil of Vaughan Williams at the Royal College of Music. Since then, there have been more than 50 recordings to date.

The Festival is well known as being the setting for the premiere of the *Tallis Fantasia*. Less well known is that eight other of Vaughan Williams' works also had their first performances in a Three Choirs Festival setting. In 1911, the Worcester audience heard his *Five Mystical Songs* for baritone soloist, chorus and orchestra for the first time, and the 1912 Festival in Hereford was the location for the premiere of the much-loved *Fantasia on Christmas Carols*. Another premiere, that of the *Four Hymns for Tenor, Viola and Orchestra*, was scheduled for the cancelled Festival of 1914.

Vera Wood, Ralph Vaughan Williams, Alice and Herbert Sumsion outside Ivor Atkins' house in Worcester during the 1938 Festival (© Richard Sumsion)

Fritz Kreisler (1875–1962), Austria-born American violinist and composer, 1913.
He was the soloist for the premiere of Elgar's *Violin Concerto*, London 1910
(© Library of Congress CC)

Subsequently, Vaughan Williams became established in the Three Choirs world and was a regular visitor, often conducting his own works. His widow later spoke of the:

> tremendous pleasure in the regular meeting each year with fellow musicians in the relaxed and festive atmosphere that prevails at the Three Choirs ... once his own contribution to the concerts was over, he was free to enjoy the parties, the receptions, the spare time, the encounters with old friends, and sometimes the simpler pleasure of *not* going to a concert ... and so it went on, with smaller or larger works every year, works by friends to be heard, enjoyed and discussed, and when the Festivals were over, perhaps a few days spent walking in the country, where the fields were golden stubble, the trees the darkest green before the first autumn touch of yellow, where apples were reddening, and where, in the pubs, beer was still beer and the bread was home-made, the cheeses local, and the Wye and Severn mirrored a landscape that had changed little since the Festivals began.

Ralph and Ursula Vaughan Williams at the 1954 Worcester Festival (© Brendan Kerney, with kind permission of the Kerney Family Creative Collection)

Over the years, as well as performing his existing works, the Festival showcased further premieres of his: *Prelude and Fugue in C minor for Organ and Orchestra* (1930, Hereford), *Magnificat* (1932, Worcester), *Two Hymn Preludes for Orchestra* (1936, Hereford), *Fantasia on the 'Old 104th'* (1950, Gloucester) and *Hodie* (1954, Worcester). As mentioned above, another premiere, that of the *Four Hymns for Tenor, Viola and Orchestra*, had also been scheduled for the cancelled (Worcester) Festival of 1914.

Incidentally, around the same time as discussions were going on between Ivor Atkins and Vaughan Williams regarding the *Magnificat* in 1932, the composer forwarded to him two Psalm settings for chorus and orchestra by the student Benjamin Britten for possible inclusion in the same Festival. These were not taken up by the Festival or anywhere else, which unfortunately helped put Britten off Vaughan Williams for life.

Since his death in 1958, Vaughan Williams' works have continued to be a feature of Festival programmes and in 2001 his *Whispers of Heavenly Death*, composed in 1908 but only rediscovered in 2001, received its first public performance at the Festival in Gloucester of that year.

7

Herbert Howells

Gloucester Cathedral: 5 September 1922

On Tuesday morning 5 September 1922 Herbert Howells made his Three Choirs composing and conducting debuts. His 'Phantasy for Orchestra' Sine Nomine, his first major commission, was scheduled in a concert before that old Festival favourite, Elijah. *A local boy, and former pupil of the Gloucester organist, Herbert Brewer, he went on to study at the Royal College of Music and become a leading composer, particularly for the church, and teacher, and a regular visitor to the Three Choirs Festival.*

Invited by Elgar

THE COMMISSION WAS in large part due to the influence of Elgar. Over the years after the 1910 Festival, Howells' relationship with the older composer had developed and matured – particularly after, as his biographer Paul Spicer reports, Howells grew to be fed up with the number of times he was being introduced to Elgar and Elgar not recognising him. Apparently, he finally said as much to Elgar's face. After that, Elgar was encouragement itself, and after being asked by Brewer for advice on up-and-coming composers, Elgar responded that 'it would be a first class thing for the festivals to get in real new blood and away from the heavy dullness of the – well you know'. He went on: 'Whatever they do has some vitality and grip ... these young men will ... do away with the remnant of the notion that everything must be a sort of Ch of E. propaganda'.

Herbert Howells (1892–1983) was a local Gloucestershire lad. He began music lessons in 1905 with Herbert Brewer, the organist of Gloucester Cathedral, and at 16 became his articled pupil at the cathedral alongside Ivor Novello and Ivor Gurney (© Howells Society)

Elgar subsequently invited a number of musicians including Howells, Arthur Bliss, Anthony Bernard, Eugene Goossens, John Ireland and Billy Reed to lunch at the Royal Societies Club in December 1920. Howells unfortunately could not attend, but Bliss later recalled that:

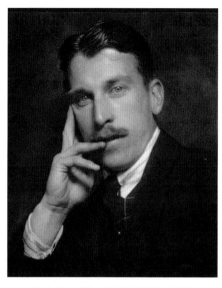

Sir Arthur Bliss (1891–1975) c.1922
(© National Portrait Gallery, London)

> The luncheon went a bit awkwardly with Elgar at his most nervous; then, when the coffee came, he suddenly told us the reason of our being gathered there. He wanted Howells, who was not present, Goossens and myself each to write a new work for the Gloucester Festival of 1922: no limitations on the form of the new works were imposed.

Subsequently, having obtained the support both of the meeting and the composers, Elgar encouraged Brewer to commission new works from them. This being the first Gloucester Festival after the war, Brewer had already been thinking about making the Festival 'essentially British' and did so. His predecessor as Gloucester organist, friend and supporter, Charles Lee Williams, had recently taken over the chairmanship of the commissioning Gloucester executive committee, which immediately rubber-stamped all the suggestions. And as Brewer proudly points out in his memoirs, 'no less [sic] than twenty-seven works by British composers' appeared in the final programme.

Savours of plainsong

Howells responded to the challenge by composing what his and Bliss's biographer, Paul Spicer, describes as 'a fascinatingly original work'. *Sine Nomine* (Latin for 'without name') is around 12 minutes long, and is an unusual concept and interesting on several levels. Howells himself in the first programme notes describes it as a Phantasy, chiefly orchestral but with parts for organ and two solo voices as well as a brief choral section at the end. He described the main theme of the work as 'savours of plainsong' (which can roughly be regarded as the folk music of the Church) and he concluded by saying that the voices should be listened to solely for what they contribute to the musical content of the piece. Scored for large orchestra, two wordless soloists (soprano and tenor) and wordless choir, in a different way it mirrors Vaughan Williams' marriage

Herbert Howells in 1922
(© Howells Society)

of ancient and modern in the *Tallis Fantasia*. Like its predecessor, it was also composed to exploit the acoustics of Gloucester Cathedral.

Scheduled before *Elijah*

Howells' debut was scheduled for the Tuesday morning in the cathedral, immediately before that Festival favourite, *Elijah*. In Brewer's defence, Howells' piece wasn't included in an early version of the programme so might have had to be slotted in somewhere at the last minute – Howells was very busy at this time.

But before Howells' debut, the audience was treated to Elgar's arrangement of the National Anthem. A suitably patriotic, British start to the concert and maybe something of a balance to the major German work that was to conclude it.

And then Howells stepped up to conduct. *Sine Nomine*'s use of wordless soloists had perturbed one of their number, which led him to ask Howells to supply words for the music just before the first performance. Howells wasn't keen, but as a compromise he gave them words from the Vulgate (a Latin translation of the Bible authorised by the Roman Catholic Church) for that performance. They were never included in the full score. The same uncertainty hung over the chorus's participation, and in the end Howells made the lower parts wordless and gave the sopranos and altos 'ora' (pray) to sing. At the final rehearsal, Elgar sensed that Howells was becoming increasingly harassed and offered him time that been allocated for the rehearsal of his works. Needless to say, Howells was extremely grateful and also enormously touched by the words of encouragement Elgar gave him as he went to take his place at the podium. His performers for that first performance were the soloists Carrie Tubb and John Coates, the Festival chorus and the London Symphony Orchestra with its leader Billy Reed.

The audience reaction can be gauged by this passage taken from *The Times* review:

> When many hundreds of people have come together to share in a certain and well-defined experience the interpolation of something so totally different as this, a piece of modern impressionistic music with voices used instrumentally and singing nothing in particular in the way of words, is apt to be received unsympathetically. The audience which comes to *Elijah* comes primarily to hear Elijah call down fire from Heaven, bring rain on the earth, and do other mighty works. It is because Mendelssohn has made all these things so graphic that they can never hear his music often enough. They naturally ask what Mr Howells is about and find that he has taken particular pains not to tell them. He does not, in fact, wish it to be about anything – he only wishes to make music.

The reviewer though did add that, 'Yet there is much that is beautiful in it, and a little that is strange, perhaps not quite enough to ears which have become used to what is vaguely described as "the modern idiom"'.

The press: a mixed response
Howells himself later recalled that his 'patient audience had to endure while it waited for the brilliant certainties of *Elijah*'. And the *Annals* only reported that, 'A new short orchestral *Phantasy* by Mr Herbert Howells preceded the *Elijah*'.

Other press opinion was also mixed. *The Musical Times* reviewer asserted that: 'It was hardly discreet to out it before an *Elijah* audience, who would be unlikely to give it a very patient or intelligent hearing'. *The Daily Telegraph* reviewer commented that:

The composition seemed more concerned with colour than with emotion or mood, and, viewed in this light, it contains much that concerns careful consideration. Mr Howells' easy command of modern orchestral and harmony devices is undeniable, as are also undeniable one or two not specially nervous weaknesses, due in part, at least, to the fact that we are going through a period of transition. To express one's ideas briefly and pointedly is a great art which Mr Howells has not fully mastered so far.

The Morning Post added:

On no possible grounds can the composer be accused of being commonplace. With his consecutive fourths, added sixths, harsh progressions of the choral masses, weird wailings of the solo voices, and the shimmering suggestiveness of the whole, Mr Howells produces a curiously ethereal effect.

The *Daily Mail* waded in with:

'Sine Nomine' it is called, no doubt because we are supposed to listen to sheer music, unpreoccupied with any verbal suggestions. This is a sign of a turn of the musical tide after many musicians during a couple of generations had sought to recommend themselves by merely adorning words, by being intensely loyal to the poets and imaging that a good libretto was three parts of a good opera. Mr Howells has gone to the point of giving his singers no words, or at least of keeping them a secret. This added to the sense of mystery evoked by those singularly beautiful pages of his. There was great cunning in the constructive art that made a longish symphonic piece grow vigorously and elaborately from a seed that looked small. This music was new enough to be worth doing; it had a natural freshness and force, and wordless song, which usually seems artificial, justified itself this time.

Locally, the *Gloucester Journal* was also more positive, saying: 'Possibly with a more intimate acquaintance we should grow acclimatised to the atmosphere of this ultra-modern orchestration and become even more enamoured of it'. But it wasn't to be heard again anywhere until 1992 when one of Howells' biographers, Paul Spicer, produced a new edition which was performed at the Three Choirs Festival of that year. This time no words were sung, as Howells had originally intended.

At lunch immediately following the performance of Bliss' *A Colour Symphony* a couple of days later, Howells later recalled how a trumpeter from the orchestra said to him: 'well young man, after the Symphony this morning even *Sine Nomine* seems tolerable!'

A showcase for British music: the rest of the Festival
The 1922 Festival was deliberately planned to showcase British music. Alongside the Howells commission, Bliss brought his radically new *A Colour Symphony*, and Goossens, *Silence*. Neither was particularly understood by the Festival audience or to Brewer's taste. The writer of the *Annals* wasn't impressed either:

A performance inside Gloucester Cathedral during the 1922 Festival. Howells' debut of his 'Phantasy for Orchestra' *Sine Nomine* was scheduled for the Tuesday morning in the cathedral immediately before that Festival favourite, *Elijah* (© The British Library Board)

We all know that feeling of restless impatience which appears when the hall clock indicates 10.25pm and four more pieces to go! It is not often (especially in Gloucester Cathedral) that new compositions beget a distinct impression of supreme boredom. But one must confess that the two compositions of Mr Arthur Bliss and Mr Eugene Goossens contained such terribly harsh progressions and positively ugly idioms of the ultra modern school that opinions were freely expressed about the propriety of admitting such music into the programme for the Cathedral, where at any rate we may hope and expect to be edified by music suitable to the solemn and mysterious atmosphere of religious exaltation. The *Colour Symphony* by Mr Bliss and the *Silence Poem* by Mr Goossens are obviously 'experiments' for secular concert halls only.

The reassuringly more traditional Three Choirs fare was also present, however, including a rare post-war Elgar premiere, and the only one hosted by Gloucester. This was a transcription for orchestra of Bach's *Fantasia and Fugue* in C minor. There were also performances of Elgar's *Apostles* and *Kingdom*, Brahms' *Symphony in D*, extracts from Wagner's *Tristan und Isolde*, Verdi's *Requiem* and Brewer's own work *The Holy Innocents*, and closing with the universally familiar and reassuring *Messiah*.

The Festival also included the unveiling of the Hubert Parry memorial in the cathedral. This was the first Gloucester Festival to be held since his death in 1918, and several pieces by him were performed over the course of the Festival.

Howells and the Festival

Howells was born in Lydney, Forest of Dean in 1892. As referred to above, he was a pupil of the Gloucester organist, Herbert Brewer. Initially a piano pupil, but from 1909 an articled pupil training to be a professional church musician. Hearing a performance of *Messiah* at the 1907 Gloucester Festival had a profound effect on him, as he first realised the dramatic power of massed voices in a vast acoustic. And as Brewer's pupil he would have played a supporting role for the 1910 Gloucester Festival, alongside his pupil colleagues, including Ivor Gurney, as referred to in Chapter 6. After leaving Brewer and Gloucester in 1912, he went on to study at the Royal College of

Music under Stanford, Hubert Parry and Charles Wood, winning most of the awards available to him. But with his family and girlfriend being local, he made frequent trips back to Gloucestershire and Gloucester, kept in touch with Brewer and also became particularly close friends with ex-Gloucester chorister, Herbert Sumsion. Sumsion had become an articled pupil of Brewer in 1915, and went on to take over from him as organist in 1928. While at the Royal College, Howells introduced Sumsion to Parry who, as Sumsion later recalled, 'on hearing that Herbert had with him a young music student from Gloucester, rushed down from the rostrum to shake me warmly by the hand – as if I were the VIP and not the other way round.'

In 1917, Brewer commissioned the orchestral miniature *Puck's Minuet* for the Gloucestershire Orchestral Society and Howells dedicated it to Brewer's young daughter, Eileen. This piece proved popular and in 1919 was programmed by Henry Wood for the Promenade Concerts, where, as Howells later reported, 'little *Puck* had so delighted the people gathered at the Queen's Hall that it had to be repeated immediately ... a most unusual occurrence'. Also in March 1919 Howells reports in his diary that:

> This morning I sat in the Library in Gloucester, helping Herbert Sumsion with his first little efforts at composition. The things he showed me reeked of Schumann-a-l'enfant and the organ loft. But he will advance rapidly with help. He has stuff in him – as a musician ...

The two continued to be close friends, and in 1940 Howells dedicated his *Six Pieces for Organ* to Sumsion. These include *Master Tallis's Testament*, which Howells regarded as a 'footnote to Vaughan Williams' *Tallis Fantasia*' that he had heard in Gloucester Cathedral at the 1910 Festival, and was one of his favourite compositions.

Back in 1915, Howells had been diagnosed with Graves' disease and given just a few months to live. But since doctors believed that it was worth taking a chance on a previously-untested treatment, he became the first person in the country to receive radium treatment, and he subsequently recovered. He was briefly assistant organist at Salisbury Cathedral in 1917, though his severe illness cut this appointment short. In the 1920s and 1930s, Herbert Howells' compositional output focussed chiefly on orchestral and chamber music, including two piano concertos; although, after joining the teaching staff of the Royal College of Music, and marrying in 1920, he didn't have the time to spend composing and his output suffered from then on as a result.

Regular visitor

Howells was nonetheless a regular visitor to the Three Choirs Festival, and in his lifetime contributed a further five new works. His works continue to be regularly programmed. Brewer returned to him for the next Gloucester Festivals of 1925 and 1928. These resulted in *Paradise Rondel* (1925) and *In Green Ways* (1928). *Paradise Rondel* was a short instrumental piece inspired by the Cotswold village of the same name, and was also notable for being included in the first Three Choirs concert to be broadcast live on the BBC. As well as being premiered at the 1928 Festival, the song cycle *In Green Ways* was programmed again for the following year's Festival. It also featured in the 1929 Promenade Concerts. Howells later described that the work grew out of a desire to illustrate five moods concerning the countryside.

The year 1950 saw the premiere of Howells' large scale *Hymnus Paradisi*. Set for chorus, orchestra and two soloists, it resulted from the sudden death of Howells' young son, Michael, from polio in 1935 and is, in effect, a requiem. As he later said, it started out as 'a personal, private document'. It was completed in 1938 and remained a private document for 12 years. At this point, Herbert Sumsion approached Howells and asked if he had anything new which the forthcoming Gloucester Festival could perform. As Sumsion later reported:

> ... he told me about a work which he had written over a period of years, and which for him had very deep significance. It was written in memory of his son Michael who had died suddenly after an illness of only a few days whilst on a visit to Gloucestershire ... our two families spent the following Christmas together at our house in Gloucester and my wife and I knew how deeply they were suffering. It was many years before Herbert was able to become reconciled to his loss ... I therefore understood that he could scarcely bear the thought of a public performance. However, he played the work to me and even on a first hearing I was deeply moved by it.

Howells left the score with Sumsion who later showed it to Gerald Finzi. Finzi then wrote to Howells saying, 'it is exciting that we shall be hearing it at Gloucester next September'. And that seems to be how the decision was made. After Sumsion and Finzi had expressed their enthusiasm, Howells asked Vaughan Williams and Adrian Boult for their opinions. They convinced Howells that the work should now have a public performance. So in that same year Howells conducted the first performance at that year's Three Choirs Festival in Gloucester on the 15th anniversary of Michael's death. It went on to be programmed at the 1951 and 1952 Festivals.

Missa Sabrinensis premiered at the 1954 Festival. Written for chorus, orchestra and four soloists, Howells later described it as not designed for ritualistic use, but it was essentially his personal and creative reaction to a text of immense, immemorial significance. The first performance was broadcast from Worcester Cathedral and privately preserved on acetate discs, representing the only recording of Howells conducting his own work.

The final Howells premiere in his lifetime was a *Festival fanfare* for brass, percussion and organ he composed to lead into Elgar's version of the National Anthem during the opening service of the 250th Festival in 1977. For this he was offered a fee of £50. He subsequently wrote in his diary for 21 August that the *Fanfare* was 'managed decently' and that the Bishop of Tewkesbury, who was a fellow Forester, winked at him during the procession.

In 2021, as a result of research by Howells scholar Jonathan Clinch, the pianist Matthew Schellhorn brought three manuscripts to first performance at that year's Festival. These were *Harlequin Dreaming*, *Phantasy* and *Petrus Suite* and date from his earliest composing. They were discovered in the special collections of the Royal College of Music and private collections.

In addition, at that Festival, Howells' *Cello Concerto*, realised from sketches by Jonathan Clinch and previous work by Christopher Palmer, was given its

Herbert Howells' *Fanfare* cover, 1977 (© Howells Society)

Herbert Howells conducting a rehearsal of *Hymnus Paradisi* at the 1977 Festival
(© Robert Garbolinski)

public performance premiere. It is a work that Howells began to sketch in 1933. Following the tragic death of his young son Michael in 1935, he turned to composing as a means of dealing with his grief, focussing on the *Cello Concerto* as well as *Hymnus Paradisi*. With the latter, he returned to it each year around the anniversary of Michael's death.

Howells continues to be a presence at the Festivals, as one of its leading home-grown composers.

GUSTAV   HOLST

8

Gustav Holst

Gloucester Cathedral: 9 September 1925

On Wednesday 9 September 1925 Gustav Holst's The Evening Watch *was premiered in a full programme that also included major works by Ethel Smyth, Elgar and Vaughan Williams, all of whom, bar Holst himself, were present to conduct their own music. However, it wasn't the first time his works had been performed at the Festival, and in 1921 he had been present at the Hereford Festival to conduct his* Hymn of Jesus, *and indeed his first Festival experience had been way back in 1893 when he heard Bach's* Mass in B Minor *for the first time. It was a life-changing experience for him. More of that later. But first his 1925 premiere.*

A troubled history

HOLST BASED THE text of *The Evening Watch*, (Op 43 No 1), on *A Dialogue* by the English metaphysical poet Henry Vaughan (1622–95). It imagines a conversation between a body and a soul, and is set for mezzo soprano and tenor solos and an unaccompanied eight-part mixed choir. The 'body' is represented in turn by the soloists, and the 'soul' by the full choir. Holst included a short footnote which states that 'there should be no variation from sempre pp [always very quiet] until near the end', hopefully to ensure that the music sustained a detached purity throughout.

The piece had a troubled history. One of two motets (there were originally more planned), Holst later claimed that he had composed them both when he was ill – he had a prolonged absence from his teaching roles in 1924–5 due to mental exhaustion – and that he could not make up his mind about

Gustav Holst (1874–1934) by Herbert Lambert, 1921. His *The Evening Watch* was premiered at the 1925 Festival (© National Portrait Gallery, London)

them. After giving it due consideration, Novello decided against publishing *The Evening Watch*, owing to its limited appeal for audiences and complex nature that would put it beyond the skills of most choirs. Both motets (the other was *Sing me the men*) were published by Curwen in 1925, who then let them go out of print. Faber republished them in 1965, and their worth began to be reassessed in the light of developments in music in the second half of the twentieth century.

The Evening Watch was actually given a first airing alongside *Sing we the men* by singers from Morley College and St Paul's Girls' School – Holst had taught at both until 1924 when he left Morley College – at the 1925 Whitsunday services at All Hallows Church, Barking. As the initial keeper of his reputation, Holst's daughter, Imogen, was keen that the official public premiere should be considered this one at the Three Choirs Festival, and this is backed up by the report of the occasion in the *Morley Magazine*:

> ... As was the case last year, the clergy of All Hallows, Barking, were kind enough to invite us to provide the music for the Sunday services, and they permitted us to rehearse on the Saturday and Sunday afternoons. After the morning service, Vaughan Williams' Mass was sung, and after the evening service several numbers from the Bach Mass were performed by choir and orchestra. Small as our forces were they were fairly well balanced. During the afternoon we had the pleasure of practising under the composer's direction, two new motets by Mr. Holst.

So, practising rather than performing. And the other music referred to is not exactly beginners' material; and indeed Vaughan Williams had dedicated the Mass referred to, his *Mass in G minor*, to Holst and his Whitsuntide singers just a few years earlier, in 1921.

Second on the bill

Attending this concert, like many of the time, took a major commitment. Starting at 11.30 in the morning, it ran through until 3.50 in the afternoon with an interval of over an hour for lunch. Holst's *The Evening Watch* was second on the bill in the second half, after Ethel Smyth had conducted two movements from her *Mass in D*. And after the four minutes of Holst, Elgar came to the rostrum to conduct his *First Symphony*. Earlier in the day, the first half of the concert had begun with a motet by Orlando Gibbons, *O clap your hands*, followed by a revival of Parry's *Job*, Walford Davies conducting his new work, *Men and Angels* and Vaughan Williams conducting a section of his *Sea Symphony*. It was a mixed bag, and a lot for the audience to take on board – and for the chorus to tackle.

Singers not at ease
As the *Sheffield Daily Telegraph* later reported:

> No one could accuse Dr Brewer's [Herbert Brewer, that year's Festival director] programme of lack of variety, and no sooner had Dame Ethel left the platform than we were plunged from a musical style tracing its lineage to Beethoven and Brahms into the experimental modernities of Holst. His *Evening Watch* ... performance was notable for the way in which the chorus attacked what was surely a highly ungrateful task.

Other reviewers also focussed on the difficulties faced by the chorus. The *Manchester Guardian* reported that:

> It was said that the work had been studied at first a great deal by the voices separately, and one would not be surprised if the singers had been obliged not only to learn it separately, but to perform it with wool in their ears so as to concentrate on their own parts ...

The Times thought that:

> Though it was well sung we could not feel that the singers were really at their ease, and it will only be when they have got over their discomfort that the hearers can be expected to find the heart of the music. We were left wondering whether it were art or artifice.

And the *Daily News* commented that, 'The motet was treated in gingerly fashion by the chorus, who however, sang creditably'. The *Birmingham Post* reviewer believed that the performance: 'was more of a triumph for Dr

Brewer and his singers than for its composer'. *The Evening Watch* could be said to have had a mixed response then. The *Daily News* followed up its comment on the chorus with:

> The piece was, to be frank, a trial to the ears but at the same time Holst seems to know where he is going, and in the meantime has the merit of making the listener alert and self-questioning. Sir Walford Davies's new work sticks more to the beaten track ...

So, not entirely negative. Indeed, *The Daily Chronicle* reviewer positively enjoyed it: 'A little new piece by Holst is of rare quality. The music reflects all the mysticism of the poem with passages of ethereal beauty, and harmonies of a novel and beautiful kind. Of some difficulty, it was finely sung by the chorus'. On the other hand, the most negative of the responses probably came from *The Daily Telegraph* describing it as:

> a setting of Henry Vaughan's 'Dialogue Between the Body and the Soul' recalling in a distinct way the dialogue between Gerontius and the Angel. The music, however is very far from recalling Gerontius or anything else. It is typical Holst. I wish I could say Holst at his best. But it may be doubted whether it is really worthwhile to attempt to make an orchestra of the choir and secure effects which leave us perplexed as to their real worth. In *The Evening Watch* Mr Holst does make his points, but not with the warmth which glows in the *Hymn of Jesus*. One might almost believe that the Dialogue takes place, not during the brief moment of parting, but during some séance held for purposes of research. The performance was far from flawless, and there were moments when to dissonance was added faulty intonation. If the work is as difficult as it sounds these failings are not surprising.

Overall, as the composer's latest biographer, Michael Short, notes:

> Although the work was given a polite reception by the audience, its austere and transcendental atmosphere was far removed from the kind of music normally to be heard at the Festival, and many listeners were disconcerted.

The journal *Musical Opinion* noted:

The new motet ... finds Holst carrying the use of unresolved dissonances to
a degree within which the very nature of all we have hitherto understood
by the word 'music' seems to be consumed ... Nobody liked Holst's music,
so far as could be discovered, and there seemed no reason why anybody
should like it.

Like the *Daily News*, *The Musical Times* compared *The Evening Watch*
unfavourably with Charles Wood's *Glory honour and laud* whose first
performance was given during the Thursday morning concert, conducted
by the composer. Apparently 'finely sung by one of the best choruses that
Gloucester has ever mustered', the reviewer pointed out that Holst's work:

is another unaccompanied Motet, but it is distinctly modern in idiom,
and while allowing for the fact that its strangeness made the performance
wanting in ease, as if the singers were not sure of their ground, one is
inclined to doubt whether with the most accurate performance it could
ever produce an effect commensurate with the means employed.

Clearly Brewer did his best in training and conducting the chorus to sing
it, but it was to neither of their tastes.

Reaction to the other items in the concert was generally positive.
According to the *Annals*, the Gibbons motet 'was heard with interest
and sung unaccompanied by the chorus with much enthusiasm'. The *Job*
revival 'seemed to be the right thing in the right place, and brought back
memories of the composer, who conducted the first performance many
years ago in Gloucester Cathedral'. *Men and Angels* was apparently 'well
received' and,

a movement from Dr Vaughan Williams' *Sea Symphony* was heard under
the same impressive conditions [in the cathedral] ... and direction of
the composer, who was welcomed as the son of an old and distinguished
Gloucester family.

Ethel Smyth's presence was also commented on: 'A novelty had been the first appearance of a lady composer-conductor in Dame Ethel Smyth'. And Elgar's *First Symphony* came with the comment that:

Excellent renderings of Sir Edward Elgar's compositions under the composer's direction were again given in the cathedral, where that welcome though solemn and mysterious atmosphere adds so much to compositions.

For *The Musical Times*, the highlight – not only of the concert but of the whole Festival as its most interesting choral premiere – was the new Walford Davies, and the journal gave several column inches of space to discussing its merits. *The Musical Times* agreed with the *Annals* about *Job*, calling it, 'a well-chosen revival of a work written for Gloucester in 1892, and containing in Job's Lamentation and the choral setting of the Almighty's response, some of his best music'. And it declared the *Sea Symphony* was 'a work of enduring value'. Ethel Smyth, it felt, 'directed an excellent performance of the Kyrie and Gloria from her *Mass in D*, which for the first time I understand, was heard in the proper environment of a cathedral'. Having noted that Elgar 'was, as usual, the most prominent personage in the programme', the reviewer commented that:

a still more welcome feature was the reappearance of one of his Symphonies, the first in A flat, which has not been heard at these festivals since its performance at Gloucester in 1910. It was not before it was due, and one renewed acquaintance with what is undoubtedly a great work with satisfaction ...

The rest of the 1925 Festival
Overall, the 1925 Festival was undoubtedly the high point of Brewer's career, not only musically speaking with its varied programme, but there were also new peaks in both attendance (19,973) and receipts. In addition, the number of stewards was a record 434, and profits from all sources amounted to £3,700 – which, because Brewer had been able to persuade the tax authorities to exempt the Three Choirs from entertainment tax, was handed in its entirety to the charity. As he pointed out in his memoirs, the attendance

The *Gloucester Journal* from 12 September 1925 showing the view inside the cathedral during the Festival, and Herbert Brewer with the composer Ethel Smyth, who was there conducting the overture to her opera *The Wreckers* (© The British Library Board)

figure of 19,973 did not include those present at the Sunday opening service or the daily services, which he estimates at around 4 or 5,000. *The Musical Times* noted his contribution:

> more than a conventional word of acknowledgement is due to Dr Brewer, who, beyond his more obvious task as conductor, had done so much to arrange the programme, organise the performances, and maintain local enthusiasm at a high pitch.

At the 1925 Festival there were more new works than ever before. Thirty-four British composers, 25 of them living, were represented in the programmes and services. Fifteen conducted their own works. There were in addition ten 'novelties' (premieres). Brewer had hoped that Sibelius would attend and conduct a new symphony as he had previously indicated he would, but he was unable to do so and a performance of his *Finlandia* was given instead. But, as noted above, Parry's *Job* was revived, the tercentenary of Orlando Gibbons was celebrated, and there were excellent Elgar renderings under the composer's direction, and a movement from Vaughan Williams' *Sea Symphony* was performed under the composer's direction.

Brewer goes on to note:

> Following the excellent example of Hereford set many years ago the Gloucester Stewards decided to give a second secular concert in Shire Hall on the Friday, and were more than justified in their decision by the room being sold out some days in advance.

Both of these secular concerts were broadcast by the fledgling BBC. As Brewer again notes, 'Broadcasting was another innovation … In this way the humblest citizen of Gloucester had the opportunity of 'standing room' at a Three Choirs Festival without fee or discomfort'. It is often thought that Brewer's son Charles was responsible for these broadcasts. In fact, Charles did not join the BBC staff until 1926 so they were entirely the result of Brewer and the reputation of the Festival.

Also, during the interval of the Wednesday evening concert at Shire Hall, Sir Hugh Allen unveiled a memorial tablet to Hubert Parry, who for the

1910 Festival had helped pay for an extension to the concert hall. Sir Hugh pointed out that this was the first occasion a Three Choirs concert had been accessible in a way which Sir Hubert could not foresee, since thousands of people all over the British Isles and beyond were listening to it via wireless, via London. This epoch-making concert included Ethel Smyth conducting the overture to her opera *The Wreckers* and Herbert Howells conducting his new work *Paradise Rondel*. Frederick Delius, 329 miles away in Grez-sur-Loing, listening on a neighbour's wireless set, heard his *On hearing the first cuckoo in spring* broadcast live from Gloucester during the Friday concert. And it is most likely that Holst listened in to his *Marching Song* from *Two songs without words*, which was on the same bill. For those unable to attend the concerts in person or have access to a wireless set, loudspeakers were also positioned in various places across the country and in Gloucester itself, proving a great attraction to the crowds of people who gathered around them to listen to the concerts. Among the local locations for the speakers was the County Electrical and Wireless Stores Limited, 86 Southgate Street, Gloucester – where, according to the *Gloucester Citizen*, 'a large company assembled at the invitation of the proprietors'.

As ever, *Messiah* drew the largest audience of the week – 3,410 tickets were sold. As Brewer conducted the 'Amen' chorus unrestrained tears rolled down his cheeks. The emotion of the occasion? Pain? We will never know. But this was to be his last Festival as director, as he died in March 1928.

Holst and Bach's *Mass in B Minor*

Growing up as a local musician Holst would have been aware of the Festival from a young age. He first visited it in 1893 when he was then just 19, and had started as a student at the Royal College of Music in the May of that year. In the following September, just before returning to London from Cheltenham, he visited Worcester to hear a performance of Bach's *Mass in B Minor*. This was the first time he had heard the work, and it was an experience that he never forgot, and continued to reference for the rest of his life.

In particular, he was overwhelmed by the exultant choruses. In the Sanctus he suddenly experienced a feeling of floating above the heads of the audience, and found himself clutching the sides of his chair to prevent his head from bumping against the roof of the cathedral. After the concert he cycled home to Cheltenham, incoherent with excitement, and tried to tell his father what a revelation it had been. But Adolph, struggling with discouragement and disillusionment in his own life, was not responsive. However, for Gustav, the memory of that performance and the love of that work stayed with him. In a 1919 letter to his close friend Ralph Vaughan Williams, on a visit to Salonica, he felt that recalling the Parthenon to him was 'like recalling the Sanctus of the B Minor – one blushes all over. Anyway I do'.

And when he was being lined up to take over the conductorship of the Bach Choir in 1928, according to his daughter and biographer, Imogen, he longed to be able to work on the *B Minor Mass*, to build it up week-by-week, and draw out the waves of sound of the Sanctus. However, already serious health issues meant that his doctors prevented him from taking up the appointment.

That concert and the press reaction to that performance

The performance of the *Mass in B Minor* that made such an impression on the student Gustav Holst was the first ever performance of that work at the Festival, and represented a bold piece of programming. It had previously been performed in this country at Leeds only, in 1886 and 1892, and the Leeds choir who sang in those performances made up half the chorus in Worcester. Hugh Blair, the young and recently-appointed Worcester organist, was the conductor. He had probably been a strong advocate of the work's inclusion in the programme, and both *The Musical Times* and the *Annals* were impressed – both by that bold programming and the performance. The *Annals* recorded: 'A greater experiment ... was Bach's *Mass in B Minor*, and a truly splendid performance of it was given on Wednesday morning, the rendering of the majestic 'Sanctus' by the chorus being especially fine'. And *The Musical Times*:

> Wednesday's proceedings opened with Bach's *Mass in B Minor* –
> performed according to the Leeds version of 1886 and 1892. This choice of
> work was bold and somewhat risky, but, although the Conductor's *tempi*
> were again too slow in not a few movements, no case of failure resulted,
> while it will be readily understood that the music derived immense
> advantage from the place of performance. Bach's ungrateful solos – we

speak in the popular sense – were conscientiously sung by Miss Williams, Miss Hilda Wilson, Mr Houghton and Mr Watkin Mills, the artist last named acting as substitute for Mr Plunket Greene. We fear the efforts of those singers met with little appreciation, all of which, such as it was, went out to the more lively and exultant choruses. Mr Sinclair of Hereford, did capital work at the organ.

Holst's Festival debut: *Hymn of Jesus* 1921

As referred to earlier, Holst's first appearance at the Festival as a performer was when he conducted his recently-published *Hymn of Jesus* at the 1921 Festival, the premiere of that work having been given in March 1920 by students of the Royal College of Music, also under his baton. *Hymn of Jesus*

Gustav Holst and Edward Elgar at the 1921 Hereford Festival

also featured on the 1924 and 1927 programmes when Holst didn't conduct it, and 1931 and 1932 when he did. He conducted both *Hymn of Jesus* and the premiere of his *Choral Fantasia* in 1931, for which he received £10 10s.

In addition, he was approached by Brewer to provide a new work for the 1928 Festival, to be performed alongside his existing *Two Psalms*. In November 1927 he wrote to Brewer requesting that he leave the matter open until 1 February, by which time he was hoping to have ideas. At that time he had none. Brewer had suggested the idea of a prelude, which Holst had warmed to. A couple of weeks later, Holst again wrote to Brewer:

> If I succeed in writing an orchestral piece it would not necessarily be a
> prelude to the *Two Psalms* but would be something that could go well as a
> prelude. If it is written in time I would reserve the first performance for the
> Gloucester Festival on condition that I conduct it for a fee of ten guineas
> and expenses and that I have adequate time for rehearsing. Would you
> give me a date by which I ought to let you know whether the work will be
> written or no. Would February 1st be too late?

The response is not known; however, there is a postcard from Holst to Brewer dated 7 December, with the cryptic message, 'Please excuse delay. By all means tell them my Hope!' As late as April 1928, a new work was expected, and was featured in the programme, and in a press release issued at the same time. In the event, nothing new was forthcoming. Holst informed the Festival during the summer that he could not after all fulfil the request. The *Two Psalms* remained in the programme, but Holst did not conduct them.

As his daughter and biographer, Imogen, records of his Three Choirs engagements:

> On more than one occasion he had followed the remains of a Roman road
> while on his way to conduct at the Three Choirs Festival. As in all things
> he was very thorough about it, and when the track led through hedges and
> ditches, Holst would go through hedges and ditches after it. Hours later,
> he would arrive at the cathedral town, battered and dishevelled and wet to
> the skin, and would conduct his rehearsal in borrowed clothes that were
> either too large or too small for him.

This certainly happened at the 1931 Festival. After the 1921 Festival in Hereford, which had featured the music of both composers – Vaughan Williams had conducted the *Fantasia on a Theme by Thomas Tallis* for string orchestra – Holst and Vaughan Williams embarked on a walking tour of the surrounding countryside, together with a mutual friend, W.G. Whittaker.

Gustav Holst and Ralph Vaughan Williams walking in the Malvern Hills
after the 1921 Hereford Festival

Of the premiere of *Choral Fantasia*, which again had a mixed reception, Herbert Howells later recorded:

> Does Gloucester recall how, on a September day in 1931, one of the most lovely organs in Christendom scattered the faint-hearted in the first bars of a new and seemingly predestined setting of the 'Ode to Music'? Holst had come again to Bridges, Bridges had written the poem to commemorate Purcell ...

And Holst himself described the occasion: 'I was too 'wropt up' to know how the *fantasia* went, but R.V.W. was moved by it, and other things don't matter too much'. As Short notes:

> Among the 'other things' were the worst press notices he had ever had in his life. The first that he opened began: "When Holst starts his new *Choral Fantasia* with a six-four on D and D sharp below that, with an air of take-it-or-leave-it, one is inclined to leave it".

However, the Festival remained loyal to Holst, and his works have continued to be programmed over the years since his death. In 1974, Herbert Howells contributed a tribute article to the programme and *Hymn of Jesus* (described by Howells as 'his very mind and spirit in every centre of accomplished choralism') and *The Planets* were performed. Another time, Howells remembered Holst as being:

> a man who walked about as if half in a trance. He looked at one pointedly straight in the eye more than anyone else, and if asked a question gave such an answer – unexpected, fundamental – as only he could give. He had no small talk. He was extraordinarily generous-minded as far as other composers and their works were concerned, which is rare. He was *wide-*minded too, in his likes and dislikes.

Percy Hull conducting the Chorus inside Hereford Cathedral during the 1927 Festival
(courtesy of Derek Foxton)

9

Gerald Finzi
Hereford Cathedral: 9 September 1949

On Friday morning 9 September 1949 in Hereford Cathedral, Gerald Finzi's Clarinet Concerto *premiered at the Three Choirs Festival. This was his first Festival premiere; the intervention of the Second World War prevented what should have been his first,* Dies Natalis, *at the cancelled Hereford Festival of 1939.*

An informal approach

FINZI, A REGULAR Three Choirs visitor, was informally approached during the 1948 Festival to produce a new work for strings for the following year's Festival. Having enjoyed composing his *Clarinet Bagatelles* in the late 1930s, and wanting to write more for that instrument he offered instead a concerto for clarinet and strings; an offer which was accepted. And 1949 was largely given over to composing it. But when August came and it was still unfinished, his wife Joy took their young sons away on holiday to Cornwall so he could push on with it undisturbed. Ursula Wood, Vaughan Williams' future wife, was with them.

Warm and romantic qualities
Set for solo clarinet and strings, in his programme note for the first performance, Finzi described his piece as having 'grown out of the warm and romantic qualities of the solo instrument, together with its natural fluidity'. It is his first mature, three movement instrumental work; the three movements being Allegro, Adagio and Vivace, and it lasts about 30 minutes.

Gerald Finzi (1901–56) conducting the orchestral premiere of *Lo, the full, final sacrifice* at the 1947 Festival

Vaughan Williams was at the first performance and made suggestions after it, in particular for the addition of a cadenza featuring the clarinet at the end of the first movement, which had previously ended abruptly. Finzi duly added one for subsequent performances.

Between Haydn and Beethoven

The new *Clarinet Concerto* was programmed second in the Friday morning concert, after the first part of Haydn's *Creation*, and before Beethoven's *Piano Concerto in G (No.4)* and a selection from Handel's *Messiah*. As ever, a mixed bag. And, as ever, there were some leading names as soloists in all the works; and, as had long been the case, the orchestra was the London Symphony Orchestra. Frederick Thurston, just about the leading clarinettist of the day – who during his career not only gave the first performance of Finzi's work but also elsewhere of Arnold Bax's *Clarinet Sonata* and Arthur Bliss's *Clarinet Quintet* – was the soloist. This wasn't Finzi's Festival conducting debut. He was never keen on conducting at the best of times, but he accepted invitations to do so because he felt it saved rehearsal time. Sumsion was among many who had tried to teach him the basics, for him to get by.

A valuable addition to our music

Ursula Wood was with the Finzi family for the performance, as Vaughan Williams was at the Festival to conduct his *A Pastoral Symphony*. She recalled later:

> afterwards we drove out to Weobly [sic] ... it was a shining afternoon, apples glistening on the trees, the country quiet and fulfilled, summer moving into autumn. Gerald was pleased with the performance; and the next month was feeling like he'd like to do another, but saying something completely different.

The press response was enthusiastic. *The Musical Times* called it 'an attractive work which is rich and lyrical, meditative and lively by turns, but always unpretentious and engaging in what one might call the English pastoral tradition'. For the *Birmingham Daily Gazette*, 'Finzi's characteristic melodic vein is well adapted to the rich qualities of the clarinet and the soloist, Frederick Thurston, provided a distinguished exponent'. And the *Daily News*:

> It is a valuable addition to our music and to that of any country where there is so masterly an artist as Frederick Thurston to play the solo part. Finzi's writing in this work is clear and refined. The music is attractive as much as when it is stern as when it is gay. The composer conducted, Thurston played exquisitely and the strings of the London Symphony Orchestra in their best style.

In a full report, LRB in the *Western Daily Press* considered it to be:

> music of considerable intensity of feeling in each of the three movements, especially the second, a kind of poignant lament. The idiom is by no means difficult to understand, no more than say, the *Clarinet Concerto* by Arthur Bliss, and like that masterpiece, or a good string quartet, or in fact everything fundamentally sound in musical thought that eschews the luxury of full orchestral dress, the Concerto greatly transcends the relative limitations of its medium. Dissonance there is in abundance, but as in the above-mentioned *Quintet*, and in Finzi's own exquisite song cycle *Dies Natalis* its effect is expressive, not aggressive.

The rest of the 1949 Festival

Sumsion had prepared a typical programme for the time, with much with local connections, coupled with 'standards' and some contemporary music. With the latter, he had developed a strong connection with the Hungarian composer, Zoltan Kodaly, who at that Festival had his *Psalmus Hungaricus* performed during the first cathedral concert. He was programmed along-side Elgar's *The Kingdom* and Beethoven's *2nd Symphony*.

Elgar was also represented by performances of *Enigma Variations* and *Gerontius*. Vaughan Williams by his *Pastoral Symphony*, as mentioned ear-lier, and further local connections were included through Parry's *Blest pair of sirens*, Holst's *Hymn of Jesus* and Samuel Wesley's *In Exitu Israel*. There were also performances of Verdi's *Requiem*, Brahms' *3rd Symphony*, Bach's *Mass in B Minor*, Beethoven's *Violin Concerto*, Mozart's *Piano Concerto*

K466, the prelude to *Parsifal* by Wagner, and in addition there was a revival of *Quo Vadis* by George Dyson.

A Three Choirs composer since 1946

Herbert Sumsion, in his 1956 obituary of Finzi, which was reprinted in the 1981 Festival programme, wrote that Finzi had been:

> known as a Three Choirs composer since 1946 when his *Dies Natalis* was performed at Hereford. Ever since that year he has been a constant contributor to our festival programmes ... he lived in the country, took the keenest interest in flowers, fruit trees, and almost everything that had life and growth, and many is the walking tour that I have had with him. He was the ideal companion, for his memory was so vivid and his knowledge so wide ... For Gloucestershire and for the Gloucestershire countryside he had a deep affection ... he has told me many a time that his heart was in the Severn Vale and especially the country around May Hill ... I have lost my most intimate musical friend, we [The Festival] have lost a composer whose worth we admired tremendously and a man for whom we had the deepest affection ...

They had been close friends for decades, and Finzi's biographer, Diana McVeagh, believes that for Finzi, Sumsion was a friend of reciprocal worth who gave him practical help with conducting and in writing for the piano, and on occasion with a compositional problem. In return, Finzi read scores and offered suggestions for the Three Choirs. But Finzi had attended the Three Choirs even before that connection began.

Introduction to Gloucestershire

Between 1922 and 1925, Finzi lived in Gloucestershire. While he and his mother were looking for a house in the county, they stayed as paying guests of a Mrs Champion at Chosen Hill Farm, on the slopes of Chosen Hill, midway between Gloucester and Cheltenham. The place was already part of English music history for in 1916 Herbert Howells had inscribed his *A Minor Piano Quartet* to 'the hill at Chosen and Ivor Gurney who knows it', and had also composed *Chosen Tune*, which he dedicated to the singer Dorothy

Dawe whom he married in 1920. The story goes that she challenged him to compose a tune to equal the beauty of the view across to the Malvern Hills. He did so, and it was among the music played at their wedding. Howells also used to go walking there with Ivor Gurney, and later with Dorothy, as often as possible. Finzi and his mother soon moved to an old house in Painswick and he was therefore based there in time for the 1922 Festival where he heard Parry's *Blest pair of sirens*, *Ode to music*, and the *Symphonic Variations*. He also saw the tablet unveiled 'Hubert Parry – Musician', and apparently felt that was all that was needed to say. Finzi also attended the following year and spotted Elgar in the distance in Worcester Cathedral 'in stays' and he found the 'new things' (Bax, Alexander Brent Smith, Malcolm Davidson) disappointing but reported to a friend that he wasn't jealous: 'the better they are, the more I love them'.

In 1925, on the last night of the year, having recently returned to living with Mrs Champion on Chosen Hill, prior to a move to London, he climbed to the church at the top of his beloved hill as the villagers rang in the year. He looked at the frosty stars and heard the bells rising from the valleys and the plain below. Then, with the ringers, he went into the sexton's small stone cottage to enjoy the cider and singing. But it was the moment of solitude that lodged in his imagination.

By the time Sumsion took over from Brewer at Gloucester in 1928, Finzi had met the younger man and his wife Alice, liked them both, and was cheered at the appointment. In the 1930s, the Sumsions were frequent visitors to the Finzis' house, by now Beech Knoll near Hungerford in Berkshire, and 'John' and Gerald would go off on two–three day walks together. At one point they went up Snowdon, but, as Gerald later reported, 'alas we were not the first'. For George V's Jubilee in 1935, the Finzis – by now Gerald and his wife Joy, rather than he and his mother – stayed with the Sumsions in their house by the cathedral, and that night they climbed May Hill to the jubilee bonfire beacon, helping a heavily pregnant Alice to keep up. He attended the 1935 Festival, where he reported that he heard the first performance of Bax's *The Morning Watch*; 'The better Bax I think' (better than his symphonies) he later wrote. And in 1937 he reported of the Festival that it was 'so much music, so many people to see, so much rushing about', and he and Joy heard Vaughan Williams' *Dona Nobis Pacem*. However, for Gerald the

Three Choirs wasn't just about the music and meeting up with his friends, he was also an inveterate book hunter, particularly during the Three Choirs Festivals, and at his death his non-music book collection numbered over 3,000 books. At later festivals Joy used to organise daily games of rounders between the afternoon concert and evensong, to allow the young people to let off steam: 'Gerald was invariably backstop ....'

Earlier in the decade, his friend Howard Ferguson had his *Two Ballads* performed at the 1934 Festival, which Gerald went to hear, reportedly bravely driving himself alone at 30 miles per hour or less. He stayed a night or two, having refused the first offer of accommodation because his prospective hostess had a butler – 'so unnerving'.

The close friendship between the Sumsions and the Finzis continued over the years. In August 1938, they and their children had a seaside holiday at Lulworth in Dorset together. And then, in July 1940, a year into the Second World War, Sumsion arrived on the Finzis' doorstep (by now in Ashmansworth, Hampshire) 'needing a holiday and sympathetic company' as Alice, his American-born wife, had taken their sons to safety in the United States.

Composer E.J. Moeran, Peers Coetmore, Herbert Sumsion, soloist Jelly d'Arányi, Alice Sumsion, Joy and Gerald Finzi at the 1946 Hereford Festival (© Richard Sumsion)

A missed premiere: *Dies Natalis*

Just before the war, Finzi had been due to conduct the first performance of one of his most characteristic works, *Dies Natalis*, at the 1939 Three Choirs Festival.

He had begun work on it soon after discovering the seventeenth-century English poet, Thomas Traherne, in the early 1920s. He worked on the piece intermittently over the years and had composed three movements by 1926. However, with the 1939 Three Choirs Festival being held at Hereford, the birthplace and parish diocese of Thomas Traherne, he felt this was the perfect place to push for a premiere of the work. At the suggestion of composer Robin Milford, Finzi submitted a revised version which included the slow movement, 'Wonder', to Percy Hull, organist of Hereford Cathedral and director of that year's Festival. To Finzi's surprise, the work was accepted by Christmas. Gerald jokingly complained to a friend that he would be in dull company at the Festival, with Dyson, Brent Smith and W.H. Reed. 'All splendid people, but dreadful composers. Can it be 1) I'm not a splendid person but a better composer or 2) I'm a splendid person but they are better composers.' In 1939, Boosey & Hawkes had, according to Finzi, more or less agreed to publish it, provided he add a fast movement for contrast. During May that year he accordingly added 'The Rapture'. But Boosey & Hawkes then said they did not want to publish it after all. In response, Finzi refused to share the cost; but after Oxford University Press and Novello also turned it down, he agreed to stand a guarantee.

On 1 September the Finzis were at the Royal College of Music in London for the final rehearsals. As *Dies Natalis* was being sung, it was announced that the Festival was cancelled. Finzi noted the fact on his copy of the programme. It was to have been his first performance at a major occasion. He wrote in a letter to a friend:

> A more unfortunate day for publication than Sept 1st cd not have been chosen & I must resign myself to the work being a complete flop for the time being. However, it's there for the future, whatever that may be, & I was lucky enough to get as far as the 2nd rehearsal (when it sounded quite all right).

On Sunday 3 September, the day originally set for the opening service, Britain and France declared war on Germany. During the course of hostilities, Finzi's friend Howard Ferguson became involved with Myra Hess in running the National Gallery lunchtime concerts. As a result, on 26 January 1940, Elsie Suddaby gave the postponed first performance of *Dies Natalis* at Wigmore Hall. Vaughan Williams wrote afterwards 'your tune is beautiful and Elsie sang it divinely'. Finzi had told Herbert Howells prior to this first performance that it had been entirely rewritten from the early work of the 1920s.

He was invited to conduct it at the 1946 Three Choirs, and he later reported that the performance 'went alright' although he noted the difference between the strings of an orchestra and a string orchestra. He had to borrow an outfit for the day to conduct it, and 'what with Tom Scott's shirt & collar, & John's [Sumsion's] tie – together with John and four assistants to help me put things on in the right order – I got through all right'. It was also included in the 1947 Three Choirs Festival, and again Finzi returned to conduct it. The 1947 Festival was also notable for including the premiere of the orchestrated version of his *Lo, the full final sacrifice*, and his orchestration of Gurney's songs.

In September 1949, when Sumsion brought the score of Howells' *Hymnus Paradisi* to Ashmansworth (as reported in Chapter 7), Gerald immediately agreed with him that it should be produced at the next Three Choirs.

Intimations and In Terra Pax: the last few years
Gerald's life, under threat since being diagnosed with cancer of the lymph nodes and given at most ten years to live, in 1951, was to be cut short in 1956. But in the meantime, he made two more major contributions to the Festival he loved so much.

The 1950 Festival saw the premiere of his *Intimations of Immortality*, a setting of words by Wordsworth. He reported that year that the piece 'had simmered for sixteen years'. In 1938 he had told a friend that he was halfway through his choral work, and reported that it was for tenor, chorus and orchestra. In 1942, he told Vaughan Williams that the longish work he had intended to dedicate to him for his seventieth birthday lay 'on the stocks at home, two thirds finished'.

He finally finished it in 1950, just in time for that year's Festival. In the end he dedicated it to Vaughan Williams' wife Adeline. Vaughan Williams was present at one of the rehearsals and Finzi's copyist Ronald Finch heard him begin to rumble with laughter. On page 44 of the vocal score, just below the words 'the pansy at my feet' the title had been misprinted as 'Intimations of *immorality*'.

The first performance under Sumsion, with Eric Greene as soloist, was on 5 September. The Finzis packed their boys off to the Cowley Manor music party and stayed at the Festival all week. Gerald later wrote of the first performance, 'Sumsion, Eric Greene and chorus and orchestra were all at their best'. McVeagh reports that 'it was a glorious festival'. Gerald's work was in the company of friends: Parry's organ prelude in his own arrangement, Holst's *Hymn of Jesus*, Vaughan Williams' *Tallis Fantasia* and *Sixth Symphony* and the first performance of Howells' *Hymnus Paradisi*. *Intimations* was also heard at the 1951 and 1953 Festivals.

In Terra Pax (full orchestral version)

Finzi had originally begun work on *In Terra Pax* in 1951. It was not a commissioned work; nobody had requested him to write it. McVeagh believes it is 'the summation of Finzi's Paradise in pastoral England, of his quest for roots and continuity, for spiritual and enduring verities in a Romantic image of a united past and present'. Finzi completed it for his own group, the Newbury String Players, in 1954, with added voices, harp and cymbals, and scored it fully for the 1956 Three Choirs Festival. As Sumsion later recalled:

> Many ... will cherish in our memories the picture of him conducting his *In Terra Pax,* sung in Gloucester Cathedral for the first time ... I like to remember the letter that he wrote to me after the festival in which he said, 'This has been the best singing of any festival that I can remember. Right to the very end, after that magnificent performance of *Hymnus Paradisi,* the chorus remained as fresh as they were at the beginning and gave everything they were asked for. Though there was not much for them to sing in *In Terra Pax,* they sang it magnificently, and I want you to pass on my really grateful thanks and affectionate greetings to every single member of the choir – not forgetting their festival conductor'.

The last visit to Chosen Hill

In 1956, the Finzis went off to Gloucester, to 'one of the happiest Three Choirs we have ever had', according to Joy's journal. They had again stayed in the King's School house with the Vaughan Williamses, Howard Ferguson, Meredith Davies, David Willcocks and others. Friends such as Herbert Howells and Edmund Rubbra were constantly in and out, 'exhilarated by the high spirits of the young people in the house party'. Ursula Vaughan Williams later described the atmosphere as being akin to 'an end of term spree at a very lively co-ed school'. Alice Sumsion had persuaded Joy to exhibit her drawings of musicians, which were visited by around 1,000 people. Gerald conducted the full orchestral version of *In Terra Pax* and was delighted with its performance.

It was therefore no surprise that the Finzis took the Vaughan Williamses up Chosen Hill, where Gerald had stood over 30 years before and heard the bells ring in the New Year – the starting point for *In Terra Pax*. 'This is where I got the idea', he told them. While the two wives stood outside in the September sun – 'for us it was still summer, with roses in the tangled churchyard grass where the sexton's children were playing; blackberries in

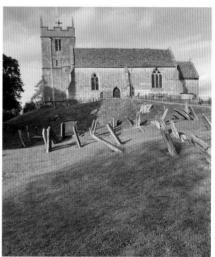

The sexton's cottage and St Bartholomew's Church at Chosen Hill where the Finzi and Vaughan Williams families walked, and where Gerald Finzi would catch the disease that would lead to his death (© Simon Carpenter)

Vaughan Williams rehearsing the chorus at the 1954 Worcester Festival
(© Brendan Kerney, with kind permission of the Kerney Family Creative Collection)

the hedges and the golden September light over the country we knew and loved' – Ursula later recounted that Gerald took 'Uncle Ralph' into the sexton's cottage. It didn't seem that important that one of the sexton's children had chickenpox. However, a couple of weeks later Finzi developed shingles, followed by chickenpox. He was taken to the Radcliffe Infirmary in Oxford where encephalitis, inflammation of the brain, was also diagnosed. He died in the hospital the next day, 27 September 1956. He was just 55 years old.

10

Applause at last

Worcester Cathedral: 24 August 1969

On Sunday evening 24 August 1969 in Worcester Cathedral, at the start of the Festival week, a centuries-long tradition was finally broken, and applause broke out in a Three Choirs Festival concert in a cathedral.

It had almost happened a few years earlier, after a performance of Walton's Belshazzar's Feast *at the 1965 Gloucester Festival. It had been the final work of the Thursday evening concert, under the baton of the Worcester organist, Christopher Robinson. The chorus had performed heroically and, in a highly-charged moment after the final 'Alleluia', a stifled cheer and ripple of applause was heard. Only a few moments long, but enough to suggest that the silent thanksgiving was not destined to last for much longer.*

The dam bursts

FOUR YEARS LATER, the era of silent appreciation finally ended. The performers who had prompted this step-change were the members of the National Youth Orchestra, and in particular their young soloist, John Miller. Applause broke out spontaneously after the Hummel *Concerto* and after each subsequent item on the programme. Critically, the audience was not a traditional Festival one, boosted as it was by parents and friends of the orchestra who had come along in order to take their siblings home after what was the last concert of a summer tour, and also official attendees from Worcestershire County Council and the County Borough of Dudley. This most probably contributed to encouraging the applause and its warmth.

The chorus at the 1954 Worcester Festival (© Brendan Kerney, with kind permission of the Kerney Family Creative Collection)

The National Youth Orchestra was directed on this occasion by Rudolph Schwarz, who by this time was combining freelancing with appointments with the Bergen and the Northern Sinfonia orchestras. His most recent appointment being chief conductor of the BBC Symphony Orchestra. He had also conducted the Youth Orchestra during their European tour of 1963. The Three Choirs concert was one of four they performed during August that year, but the only one that wasn't their own promotion. Their programme included, as well as the Hummel, Brahms' *Academic Festival Overture*, 'Jupiter' from Holst's *Planets* suite and Schubert's *Symphony No.7 in C major*.

John Miller: bright future

John Miller had joined the orchestra as a 16-year-old in 1967 and became a soloist at 18. The Three Choirs concert made a big impression on him:

> I remember the occasion with complete clarity, and it was very important to me. The applause occurred after the concerto, and I was told that that was the first time it had ever occurred in the Cathedral. I [also] remember in the interval meeting Timothy Reynish, who at the time was first horn in the CBSO, and a musician I would meet many times in the future in several capacities. Playing with Rudolf Schwarz was a formative experience

John Miller, second from left, playing with the National
Youth Orchestra in 1969 (© John Miller)

– he was a distinguished conductor, and his refined manner, his dress hair and demeanour was probably like playing with Gustav Mahler. He said a lot about shape of phrase and musical meaning, and got the orchestra to play Classical and early Romantic music in a particular way. This experience of the NYO with Schwarz and Pierre Boulez the next year pointed to a career in music that spanned five decades as a trumpeter.

John had begun his musical life playing cornet with Tullis Russell Mills Band, a community-based brass band from Glenrothes, Fife. He went on to take up trumpet playing as a career, and, at the time of the Three Choirs concert, had a bright future ahead of him. He went on to be a member of the Philip Jones Brass Ensemble (1972–80) and the Philharmonia Orchestra (1977–94). He is also a founder-member of the Wallace Collection brass ensemble. He joined the staff of the Royal Northern College of Music in 1999 as Head of Brass and was Head of Wind and Percussion 2013–17. He became a National Youth Orchestra tutor in 1991. In September 2022, his book *The Modern Brass Ensemble in Twentieth-Century Britain* was published by Boydell *&* Brewer.

Applause: why wrong for so long?

The practice of not applauding any sort of live performance now seems unbelievable, but there are reasons behind why it should have taken so long for applause to have been accepted at a Festival cathedral concert. The main one was the setting: a cathedral, and thereby in the Church's eyes, the house of God, was not considered a suitable context for applause. Therefore, from the beginning of the Festivals, all music had been received in reverent silence.

This attitude can be taken to be a legacy of the opposition to the Festival as a whole from large sections of the local Anglican church in the nineteenth and early twentieth centuries. For a long while, concerts were designated acts of worship; they were literally that in the early days, being services with orchestra and soloists. But this led to years of grumbles about payment being received for admission. It is also related to why, for so many years, 'secular' music at the Festivals, including Handel's *Messiah*, as seen in Chapter 1, were scheduled for non-ecclesiastical buildings, and why the musical programming was so conservative for so long.

This attitude was also not confined to the Festival. For a long while, until comparatively recently, applause was discouraged from any church/ cathedral-based concert.

The rest of the 1969 Festival

It was a memorable Festival – Christopher Robinson's second as director – for many other reasons. A particular highlight was that four composers, whose music was performed during the week, were present: Luigi Dallapiccola, Elizabeth Maconchy, Jonathan Harvey and William Mathias.

Performances of Luigi Dallapiccola's *Due liriche di Anacreonte* and *Quadro liriche di Antonio Machade* were given in the Monday afternoon recital at Hartlebury Castle by the Vesuvius Ensemble of London; the soprano soloist in both works was Jane Manning. Dallapiccola was present, and was also in the cathedral on Thursday afternoon to hear Christopher Robinson conduct the Royal Philharmonic Orchestra and the Festival chorus in his *Canti di Prigionia*. The work was described by one contemporary critic as:

> among the most powerful gestures of 'protest through music' ever made:
> the work may be regarded as the supreme musical symbol of all the anguish,
> suffering and frustrated idealism of the Italian people during the tragic last
> phase of the Fascist regime and the catastrophic events which followed.

Elizabeth Maconchy was present for the first performance by the three cathedral choirs and the Birmingham Brass Consort, who had commissioned it, of her *And Death Shall Have No Dominion*. This piece made a lasting impression on Adrian Partington, then a Worcester chorister, and in 2020 he revived it with the BBC National Orchestra and Chorus of Wales. In addition, the premiere of a setting of Psalm 150 by William Mathias was given in the opening service. Among visitors to the Festival were Edward Heath, then leader of the opposition, accompanied by Worcester MP, Peter Walker.

More applause, but not for Beethoven

There was no applause after the Monday evening performance of Beethoven's *Missa Solemnis*, but on the Tuesday afternoon there was a single outburst of clapping after Richard Lloyd had conducted Peter Maxwell Davies's *Five Carols* for boys' voices. More persistent applause was heard on Tuesday evening for Stravinsky's *Symphony of Psalms* and the premiere of Jonathan Harvey's *Ludus Amoris,* the first work commissioned by the Festival with funds provided by the Arts Council. In fact, the Festival audience gave *Ludus Amoris* a near-frenzied reception, and subsequently the orchestra manager asked Christopher Robinson if he would bring the Festival chorus to the Festival Hall to perform it again the following June. This duly went ahead and was received well.

On Wednesday, the audience was strangely silent following Rossini's effervescent *Petite Messe Solennelle.* But both of Thursday's concerts were applauded. In the first there were performances of Bach's *Brandenberg Concerto No.2*, Handel's *Utrecht Te Deum*, Rossini's *Sonata in G for strings* and Dallapiccola's *Canti di Prigonia*. The evening concert included Dvořák's *Te Deum*, Schubert's *Symphony No.3* and Janáček's *Glagolitic Mass*.

However, Adrian Boult requested no applause for Friday's afternoon concert by the Royal Philharmonic Orchestra, so none followed performances of Malcolm Williamson's *Overture Santiago d'Espado*, Elgar's *Violin Concerto* (soloist Hugh Bean) and Schumann's *Symphony No.1*. It is not recorded whether applause was heard after the final performance of the week, that of Elgar's *The Dream of Gerontius* on the Friday evening.

Outworn tradition nearly ditched

Adrian Boult's request for no applause for the Friday afternoon concert was met with much disappointment by the local press: 'The audience were getting used to clapping ... and applause at a concert to be broadcast ... would have ditched the outworn tradition once and for all', as the *Hereford Times* reported. Kenneth Dommett in his *Birmingham Post* report for the whole Festival included, 'I am pleased incidentally to see that the opposition to applause at these concerts is now almost overcome'.

However, not everyone agreed that applause in the cathedrals was a welcome precedent, and a lively correspondence was carried on in the Worcester and Hereford newspapers in 1969 and 1970. Some traditionalist Festival goers were never reconciled to the change. But the momentum was too great for effective protest; the silence had been broken forever, and finally disappeared in 1972. But, as far as some clergy were concerned back in 1970, the battle wasn't yet lost, as a letter from an Oxford vicarage to *The Times* in March 1973 shows:

> One of us went to a concert on the second day [of the 1970 Hereford Festival]. Clearly there had been some applause at an earlier concert for the proceedings were opened by a cleric who made an announcement to the effect that we were reminded that the Dean and Chapter did not deem it seemly to applaud in God's house. What joy when after the splendid first item of the concert, the audience (*not* 'congregation'!) burst immediately into spontaneous and loud clapping. We don't know whether a similar announcement was made at later concerts.

Overview: the Festival at the start of the 1970s
Aside from the applause issue, the Festival was transitioning through a tricky time. A couple of years earlier, after the 1967 Festival, William Mann wrote in *The Times*:

> It is difficult to be sure in what frame of mind one should approach the Three Choirs Festival. Is it a local jollification during which, for one week, the organists of the three cathedrals try their hands at the role of Toscanini and match their choir-master-organist techniques (not necessarily those of a good conductor) against a wide stretch of the choral and symphonic repertory as they fancy? Is it, as England's oldest music festival ... to be regarded *ipso facto* as an event of national cultural importance, to be judged by the standards of, say, Glyndebourne or Edinburgh? Or a respectable shop window for all that is most worthwhile in choral and orchestral music of all countries and periods? Or do we have to admit that an existence of 240 years inevitably induces some sort of senile decay and that, in its present form, the Three Choirs Festival needs to be replaced or retired for the musical health of the country?

His views about the suitability or otherwise of cathedral organists conducting professional orchestras were not new, as has been shown elsewhere. But, over the years, more concerts were relinquished to professional conductors. Coincidence or not, but at the first Festival following this article appearing, John Sanders' first home Festival in Gloucester, the conducting load was shared by the professional conductors, Hugo Rignold, Sir Adrian Boult and Raymond Leppard, in addition to Christopher Robinson and Richard Lloyd.

New brooms in the 1950s

Of the wider criticism of the Festival's place in the musical life of the nation, there had been much recent soul searching, particularly since the arrival of the new post-war festivals which were setting new standards in performance and programming, including Aldeburgh and the local Cheltenham Festival. However, the 1950s had also seen ambitious organists in place in all three cathedrals: Meredith Davies followed by Melville Cook at Hereford, David Willcocks at Worcester and Herbert Sumsion, now the senior partner, at Gloucester. It was Meredith Davies who, unsuccessfully unfortunately, commissioned Benjamin Britten to compose a new work for the 1952 Festival, and who, at his valedictory Festival in 1955, challenged convention by programming less familiar and new music by Stravinsky, Poulenc, Bliss, Racine Fricker, Humphrey Searle, Lennox Berkely and Paul Huber. Melville Cook brought Benjamin Britten in person to the Festival for the first time to conduct his *St Nicholas* cantata and *Sinfonia da Requiem* in 1958. And it was David Willcocks who, in 1954, finally managed to persuade the dean and chapter of Worcester to allow the cathedral audience to be seated facing the performers instead of each other, across the central aisle. Formerly, there had been strong opposition to any suggestion that the audience should turn their backs to the altar. It was also down to Willcocks that William Walton's masterpiece, *Belshazzar's Feast*, with its 'racy' text and subject matter, was eventually permitted a Three Choirs performance in 1957, nearly 30 years after its publication. Sumsion, who finally obtained permission to programme a complete performance of Vaughan Williams' *A Sea Symphony* in 1962 – Walt Whitman's words were the issue here – was a lasting link with the past, and conducted music by Elgar, Holst, Howells, Finzi and Vaughan Williams, with intuitive understanding formed by a close association with the composers. He helped develop a Three Choirs understanding of their works, which continued through his pupils Melville Cook, John Sanders at Gloucester and Donald Hunt at Worcester.

At the 1951 Worcester Festival. TOP LEFT: Meredith Davies; TOP RIGHT: Herbert Sumsion; BOTTOM: David Willcocks and Sir Ivor Atkins (all images © Brendan Kerney, with kind permission of the Kerney Family Creative Collection)

On the organisational front, there was also a major development during the 1950s. In 1957 the Three Choirs Festival Association Ltd was incorporated, for the first time formally bringing together the local committees from each city. This had come about from prompting by the Arts Council when they were approached to financially help out the Festival after the 1953 event. They were anxious to assist 'but ... only ... if some constitution linking the three cities was adopted and that under such constitution no part of the proceeds from the concerts be used for charitable purposes'. This was rejected by Gloucester and Worcester, but in time all three local committees came round to the inevitable.

Post-1969 musical developments: the view of Adrian Partington

Someone who is well-placed to assess how the Festival responded to those criticisms and has developed since 1969 is the present Gloucester organist, Adrian Partington. He made his Festival debut as a Worcester chorister at the 1969 Festival, and between 1981 and 1991 was assistant organist at Worcester, before pursuing a career as a choral conductor elsewhere. In 2007 he returned to the area and the Festival when he was appointed to Gloucester.

Adrian remembers his first Festival fondly: 'I found the week to be a wonderful experience, and I can still remember an enormous amount about the Festival. In fact, I can remember more about it than I can about [more recent Festivals]!' He gives examples of some of the subsequent changes:

The chorus at the 1977 Gloucester Festival (© Robert Garbolinski)

When I was a chorister, the boys sang in everything. It was thrilling! I remember learning Beethoven's *Missa Solemnis*, Janáček's *Glagolitic Mass* and so on, and have never had to re-learn them since. One day in 1969, we sang the Three Cathedral Choirs concert at 2.30, Evensong at 5.15 and then the evening concert (Stravinsky etc.) at 7.30. That is more singing in one day than the choristers are allowed to sing *in a week* now. Times have changed.

He continues:

Other changes concerning the choristers are as follows: in 1969 there were no girl choristers, and all the boys boarded. Now the children go home after Evensong each day; they rarely stay for the evening concert. Children get far more tired through travelling than through singing. I really regret the way the choristers' contribution to the Festival has been so drastically reduced. But rules are rules.

He then turns to the main chorus:

The biggest change is its size! In 1969, the chorus was almost 300 strong; [these days] it is little more than 120. This means that there are often balance issues between chorus and orchestra these days, which simply didn't exist 50 years ago. Again, it is rules which have caused the diminution of the chorus: health and safety regulations, fire regulations, insurance regulations etc. However, I hope that the chorus is now more flexible and better organised than it was in the 1960s. Certainly the preparation is more organised.

And then to one of the initiatives:

For my first Festival as director in 2010, I insisted on two big changes. First of all, I had the dates of the Festival week brought earlier in the year so that there wasn't such a huge gap between the end of the summer term and the Festival week. I had observed when I was assistant at Worcester that the empty period after the end of term was wasted time where the Festival was concerned. And secondly, I made the chorus rehearse continuously from

May until the Festival started. Until 2010, the chorus rehearsed until the end of the private school terms in early July, and then had four to six weeks in which to forget everything. It is not surprising that performances in the old days were often scrappy affairs. I used to think in what other sphere of human activity was the preparation so separated from the performance? It was absurd, and I have never understood why none of my distinguished predecessors chose to do what I did in 2010. Anyway, everybody takes it for granted now that rehearsals continue until the Festival itself.

The view of Alexis Paterson, the Festival's chief executive 2016–24 is:

As Simon makes evident throughout this book, the Three Choirs Festival has been looking forward from the very start. From the stewards and cathedral chapters of yesteryear to the staff and trustees of the organisation today, a strong sense of custodianship and the need to nurture such an illustrious tradition still informs the decisions that are taken today. At the heart of those choices is always – and always has been – an adaptability and determination to not only survive, but to thrive, and embrace the challenges and opportunities of an ever-changing world. Who can imagine

Adrian Partington at the podium during the 2016 Festival
in Gloucester Cathedral (© Derek Foxton)

now that we'd chastise (and fine!) the lay clerks for giving their ever popular late-night secular showcases while the audience had a drink to hand (as happened to the unfortunate lay clerks at Worcester in the years just preceding the festival's start), nor that we (or the orchestra) would allow instrumentalists to be booted off stage to make way for more singers on the overstuffed chorus benches (as happened to poor old Bliss at the premiere of his – chorus free! – *A Colour Symphony*)? I'd like to think that today's festival always strives to put the music ahead of politics and personal sensitivities.

We learn; we evolve; we adapt. And above all, we continue to bring great music to this corner of the world. As all arts organisations must in the challenging era the sector faces at the time of writing, we continue to reimagine what the festival is in order to preserve the heart of its purpose. That purpose is to bring music to the region that would not otherwise be heard; to offer up the very best opportunities to sing for as many people as we can; to continue to champion the very best up-and-coming composers and performers and above all, to revel in the joy of music making, and the impact that can have on us all.

So, the Festival continues, constantly improving and reinventing itself, and now with a full-time professional office at its heart. It continues to adapt to the world around it, and to innovate, as it moves into its fourth century. As it does so, Handel's *Messiah* may now be a rarity on the programme, but at least audiences can now applaud performances guilt-free.

key figures mentioned in the text

ALBANI, DAME EMMA: b.1847. French Canadian soprano. Studied in Paris and Milan; debut Messina 1870; Covent Garden debut 1872; New York Metropolitan Opera debut 1894; retired from stage 1896 but continued to sing oratorio; retired to teach 1911. d.1930.

ALLEN, SIR HUGH: b.1869. Organist and choirmaster. Studied at Reading and Oxford; conductor of London Bach Choir 1907–20; professor of music, University of Oxford, 1918–46; director of Royal College of Music 1919–37; knighted 1920. d.1946.

ATKINS, SIR IVOR: b.1869. English organist, composer and conductor; organist Worcester Cathedral 1897–1950; composer of choral works; edited with Elgar Bach's *St Matthew Passion*, 1911; knighted 1921 for his role in reviving the Three Choirs Festival after the First World War. d.1953.

AUSTIN, FREDERIC: b.1903. English baritone and composer. Covent Garden debut 1908; principal baritone Beecham Opera; artistic director British National Opera Company 1924; composer of a symphony, symphonic poem and choral works. d.1952.

BANTOCK, SIR GRANVILLE: b.1868. English composer, conductor and educationalist. Trained at Royal Academy of Music 1889–93; music director of New Brighton near Liverpool, where he championed the music of contemporary British composers; principal of Birmingham School of Music 1900–34; professor of music Birmingham University 1908–34; knighted 1930. d.1946.

BARNBY, SIR JOSEPH: b.1838. English organist, composer and conductor. Gave annual performances of Bach's *St John Passion* when organist of St Anne's, Soho, London 1863–71; precentor Eton College 1875; principal Guildhall School of Music 1892–96. d.1896.

BAX, SIR ARNOLD: b.1883. Composer and writer. Studied at Royal Academy of Music; knighted 1937; Master of the King's/ Queen's Music 1942–53. d.1953.

BEARD, JOHN: b.1716. English tenor associated with Handel operas and oratorios. Debut in 1734 revival of *Il pastor fido*. The tenor parts of several of Handel's compositions were written with Beard in mind. He also sang in the Chapel Royal choir. d.1791.

BENNETT, SIR WILLIAM STERNDALE: b.1816. English composer, pianist and teacher. King's College, Cambridge chorister at seven, then went on to newly-founded Royal Academy of Music two years later; in 1836, visited Leipzig and became a friend of Schumann; conductor of Philharmonic Society 1856–66; conducted first English performance of Bach's *St Matthew Passion* 1854; founder of the Bach Society and also professor of music, Cambridge University from 1856; principal of Royal Academy of Music from 1866; knighted 1871. d.1875.

BERNARD, ANTHONY: b.1891. English conductor, pianist and composer. Founder and conductor of London Chamber Orchestra and London Chamber Singers, reviving much old music; conductor of Dutch Chamber Orchestra 1922–26; organist, accompanist and conductor at Shakespeare Memorial Theatre 1932–42. d.1963.

BLAIR, HUGH: b.1864. English organist, conductor and composer, and friend and supporter of Elgar. Chorister of Worcester Cathedral; organ scholar and college organist, Christ's College, Cambridge; BA 1886, BMus 1887, MA 1896, DMus 1906; assistant organist Worcester Cathedral 1887–89; organist in charge 1889–95 and organist 1895–97; directed the Three Choirs Festivals of 1893 and 1896; resigned 1897 and appointed organist of Holy Trinity Church, Marylebone; director of music of the Borough of Battersea 1900–04. d.1932.

BLISS, SIR ARTHUR: b.1891. Composer. Educated at Rugby, Pembroke College, Cambridge and Royal College of Music; war service 1914–19; professor at Royal College of Music 1921–22; USA 1923–25; m. Gertrude Hoffman 1925; director of music BBC 1942–44; chairman Music Committee of British Council 1946–50; knighted 1950; Master of Queen's Music 1953–75. d.1975.

BOULT, SIR ADRIAN: b.1889. English conductor. Began musical education under (Sir) Hugh Allen at Christ Church, Oxford; Leipzig Conservatoire 1912–13; came to prominence 1918–19 with outstanding performances of works by Elgar, Vaughan Williams and Holst, all of whom became close friends; on teaching staff of Royal College of Music 1919–30; conductor of City of Birmingham Symphony Orchestra 1924–30; music director BBC 1930–42; chief conductor BBC Symphony Orchestra 1931–50; principal conductor London Philharmonic Orchestra 1951–57; returned to Royal College of Music staff 1962–66; knighted 1937. d.1983.

BOYCE, WILLIAM: b.1711. English composer and organist. Chorister St Paul's Cathedral, London; organist of Oxford Chapel, Vere Street 1734; organist, St Michael's, Cornhill 1736 and composer to Chapel Royal; appointed Three Choirs Festival conductor 1737 for which he composed his *Worcester Symphony* and other works; DMus, Oxford 1749; Master of the King's Musick 1755; organist Chapel Royal 1758. d.1779.

BOYLE, FRANK: b.1857. English tenor. Chorister Holy Trinity Barnstable, won scholarship to National Training School of Music in South Kensington, the forerunner of the Royal College of Music; sang in Messiah at the Royal Albert Hall and at the Promenade Concerts in 1880; a soloist at the Hereford Festival of 1882; toured with D'Oyly Carte Opera Company in 1884; stayed with company off and on until 1889. d.1892.

BREWER, SIR HERBERT: b.1865. English organist, conductor and composer. Chorister of Gloucester Cathedral 1877–80; organ scholar Exeter College, Oxford 1883; studied Royal College of Music, 1883–85; organist Bristol Cathedral 1885; St Michael's Coventry 1886–92; music master Tonbridge School 1892–96; organist Gloucester Cathedral 1896–1928; knighted 1926; compositions include *Emmaus* (1910) and *The Holy Innocents* (1904). d.1928.

BRIDGE, SIR FREDERICK: b.1844. English organist, conductor and composer. Chorister Rochester Cathedral; organist Manchester Cathedral 1869–75; professor of harmony Owens College, Manchester (now University of Manchester), 1872–75; deputy organist Westminster Abbey, 1875–82; organist 1882–1918; first professor of music University of London 1903. d.1924

CARADORI-ALLAN, MARIA: b.1800. Italian-born soprano who settled in England. London debut 1822; successful career in opera but main claim to fame as chief soprano soloist in the first London performance of Beethoven's *9th Symphony* 1825 and in the first performance of Mendelssohn's *Elijah*, Birmingham 1846. d.1865

CARRODUS, JOHN (TIPLADY): b.1836. English violinist. Leader of several London orchestras including Covent Garden 1869–95; his three sons were musicians and at the Hereford Festival of 1894 they and their father all played in the orchestra. d.1985.

COATES, JOHN: b.1865. English tenor, originally baritone. Sang baritone roles with D'Oyly Carte Opera Company 1894; debut as tenor 1899; sang Faust in Gounod's opera, Covent Garden 1901; member of Moody-Manners and Beecham Opera Companies; also achieved eminence in choral works, notably Elgar's *The Dream of Gerontius*. d.1941.

COOK, (ALFRED) MELVILLE: b.1912. English organist, conductor, composer and teacher. Chorister Gloucester Cathedral 1923–28 and later articled pupil of Herbert Sumsion. Studied with Herbert Brewer and Edward Bairstow; studied at Durham University, BMus 1934 and DMus 1940; assistant organist of Gloucester Cathedral 1932–37; organist All Saints' Church, Cheltenham 1935–37; organist Leeds Parish Church 1938–56; organist Hereford Cathedral 1956–66; director Winnipeg Philharmonic Choir and organist and choirmaster at All Saints' Anglican Church, Winnipeg 1966; organist Metropolitan United Church, Toronto 1967–86; taught organ McMaster University 1974–77; retired to Cheltenham 1986. d.1993.

CROFT, WILLIAM: b.1678. English composer and organist. Organist St Anne, Soho, London 1700–12; Chapel Royal 1707 and master of the children and composer from 1708. d.1727.

CROSSLEY, ADA: b.1874. Australian contralto. Melbourne debut 1892; London debut 1895; reputation chiefly in oratorio. d.1929.

DALLAPICCOLA, LUIGI: b.1904. Italian composer and pianist. Conservatoire Cherubini, Florence 1922; in late 1920s taught, gave recitals; joined pianoforte staff of Conservatoire Cherubini 1934; fell out of favour with authorities because of his opposition to Fascism; after 1945 spent considerable amount of time in USA. d.1975.

DAVIES, MEREDITH: b.1922. English conductor and organist. Studied Royal College of Music and Academy of St Cecilia, Rome; conductor of Bach Choir 1947; organist St Albans Cathedral 1947–49; organist Hereford Cathedral 1949–56; associate conductor City of Birmingham Symphony Orchestra 1957–60; musical director English Opera Group 1962–64; conductor Vancouver Symphony Orchestra 1964–71; shared with composer conducting of first performance of Britten's *War Requiem* 1962. d.2005.

DAVIES, SIR (HENRY) WALFORD: Welsh composer and organist. Studied Royal College of Music; taught Royal College of Music 1895–1903; organist Temple Church, London 1898–1918; conductor Bach Choir 1903–07; musical director RAF 1917; professor of music University of Wales 1919–26; organist St George's Chapel, Windsor 1927; Master of the King's Music 1934–41; one of the first popular broadcasters on music; knighted 1922. d.1941.

DONE, WILLIAM: b.1815. English organist and conductor. Organist Worcester Cathedral 1844–95. d.1895.

ELGAR, SIR EDWARD: b. 1857. Leading English composer and conductor, many of whose works remain in the international classical repertoire, including the *Enigma Variations*, the *Pomp and Circumstance* marches, the *Cello Concerto*, the *Violin Concerto*, two *Symphonies* and *The Dream of Gerontius*; largely self-taught; Master of the King's Music 1924–34. d.1934.

ELLICOTT, ROSALIND: b.1857. English composer and singer. Received early musical training from her mother and S.S. Wesley in Gloucester; studied piano at the Royal Academy of Music 1874–76; studied composition at Brompton Oratory 1885–92; member of the International Society of Musicians and National Society of Professional Musicians. d.1924.

FERGUSON, HOWARD: b.1908. Irish composer, pianist and teacher. Studied pianoforte with Harold Samuel 1922 and at Royal College of Music; professor at Royal Academy of Music 1948–63. d.1999.

FINZI, GERALD: b.1901. English composer. Studied under Sir Edward Bairstow 1918–22; private pupil of R.O. Morris 1925; professor of composition, Royal Academy of Music 1930–33. d.1956.

FISCHER, CHRISTIAN (JOHANN): b.1733. German oboist. Played in Dresden Court Orchestra 1764; member of Queen's Band, London 1768; married Gainsborough's daughter 1780; returned to continent on not being appointed Master of King's Band 1786; returned to London 1790. d.1800.

GODFREY, DAN: b.1868. English conductor. Educated King's College School and Royal College of Music; founded Winter Gardens orchestra in Bournemouth (later the Bournemouth Symphony Orchestra) 1893; knighted 1922. d.1939.

GOOSSENS, SIR EUGENE: b.1893. English conductor, violinist and composer. Studied Bruges Conservatoire, Liverpool College of Music and Royal College of Music; violinist Queen's Hall Orchestra 1911–15; assistant conductor 1916–20; conducted opera and ballet Covent Garden 1921–23; conductor Rochester Philharmonic Orchestra, USA 1923–31; Cincinnati Symphony Orchestra 1931–47; director New South Wales Conservatoire 1947–56; knighted 1955. d.1962.

GREENE, HARRY PLUNKET: b.1865. Irish bass-baritone. Son-in-law of Sir Hubert Parry. Studied Stuttgart, Florence and London; sang in London concerts from 1888, opera from 1890; later confined himself to songs and oratorio; first interpreter of songs by Parry, Stanford and Vaughan Williams, some written for him; first singer of bass parts in *The Dream of Gerontius*. d.1936.

GROVE, SIR GEORGE: b.1820. English writer on music, and teacher. Trained as civil engineer, taking part in construction of Crystal Palace of which he was secretary 1852–73; became increasingly involved in music, writing programme notes for Crystal Palace concerts for 40 years; began work on *Grove's Dictionary of Music and Musicians* 1873; first director Royal College of Music 1882–94; knighted 1893. d.1900.

GURNEY, IVOR: b.1890. English composer and poet. Wrote poetry, setting several of his own poems to music as well as poetry by A.E. Houseman etc.; chorister Gloucester Cathedral 1900; articled pupil of Herbert Brewer at Gloucester Cathedral 1906–11; won scholarship to Royal College of Music 1911; joined army 1915; returned to Royal College of Music 1919, but declared insane 1922. d.1937.

HANDEL, GEORGE FRIDERIC: b.1685. German-British composer, recognised as one of the greatest composers of his age. He brought Italian opera to its highest development and created the genres of English oratorio and organ concerto and brought a new style to English church music; trained in Halle and worked as a composer in Hamburg and Italy before settling in London in 1712; naturalised British subject from 1727. d.1759.

HARVEY, JONATHAN: b.1939. English composer and teacher. Cellist in National Youth Orchestra; studied Cambridge and Glasgow Universities; studied with Babbitt 1969–70; on staff music department Southampton University 1964–77; Sussex University 1977. d.2012.

HARWOOD, BASIL: b.1859. English organist and composer. Studied Charterhouse, Oxford, BMus 1880, DMus 1896, and Leipzig; organist of St Barnabas Pimlico 1883–87, Ely Cathedral 1887–92, Christ Church Cathedral Oxford 1892–1909; first conductor of the Oxford Bach Choir 1896; precentor of Keble College, Oxford 1892–1903. d.1949.

HAYES, WILLIAM: b.1708. English composer, organist, singer and conductor. Gloucester cathedral chorister 1717–27; assistant organist Gloucester Cathedral 1727–29; organist St Mary's Shrewsbury 1729–31; organist Worcester Cathedral

1731–34; organist Magdalen College, Oxford 1734–41; BMus 1735; DMus 1749; Heather Professor of Music and organist, University Church of St Mary the Virgin, 1741; instrumental in the building of the Holywell Music Room in 1748, the oldest purpose-built music room in Europe. d.1777.

HESS, DAME MYRA: b.1890. English pianist. Studied Guildford School of Music and Royal Academy of Music; debut 1907; USA debut 1922; garnered fame during Second World War when she organised almost 2,000 lunchtime concerts at the National Gallery, London – for this she was made a dame in 1941. d.1965.

HOLST, GUSTAV: b.1874 (born Gustavus Theodore von Holst). English composer and teacher, best known for his orchestral suite *The Planets*. Educated Cheltenham Grammar School 1886–91; Royal College of Music 1893–98; trombonist with Carl Rosa opera company 1897–1903; trombonist with Scottish Orchestra 1900–03; teacher James Allen Girls' School 1904–20; teacher Passmore Edwards Settlement 1904–07; director of music at St Paul's Girls' School 1905–34; musical director of Morley College 1907–24; composition teacher University College, Reading 1919–23; composition teacher Royal College of Music 1919–24. d.1934.

HOWELLS, HERBERT: b.1892. English composer, organist and teacher. Articled pupil of Herbert Brewer at Gloucester Cathedral 1909–12; Royal College of Music 1912–17; assistant organist Salisbury Cathedral 1917, resigned due to ill health; composition teacher Royal College of Music 1920–79; succeeded Holst as director of music at St Paul's Girls' School 1936–62; King Edward VII Professor of Music, University of London 1950–64; stood in for Robin Orr as organist of St John's College, Cambridge 1941–45. Howells wrote church music throughout his life. He set *Magnificat* and *Nunc Dimittis* no fewer than 20 times and these settings represent the most significant contribution to the Anglican repertoire of the twentieth century. Particularly memorable are the settings for King's College, Cambridge, Gloucester and St Paul's. d.1983.

HULL, SIR PERCY: b.1878. English organist and composer. Chorister Hereford Cathedral, afterwards pupil of George Robertson Sinclair and assistant organist 1896–1914; appointed organist of Hereford 1918; knighted 1947. d.1968.

HUNT, DONALD: b.1930. English organist and conductor. Chorister Gloucester Cathedral, afterwards pupil of Herbert Sumsion and assistant organist 1944–54; organist St John's Church, Torquay 1954–57; organist and choirmaster Leeds Parish Church, Leeds City organist, and lecturer at Leeds College of Music 1958–75; awarded doctorate from Leeds University, *honoris causa* 1975; organist Worcester Cathedral 1976-96; principal of the Elgar School of Music in Worcester (becoming music advisor after 2007). d.2018.

IRELAND, JOHN: b.1879. English composer and pianist. Studied Royal College of Music 1893–1901; organist St Luke's, Chelsea 1904–26; professor of composition Royal College of Music 1923–39. d.1962.

JAEGER, AUGUST: b.1860. German musician and publisher. Head of publishing, Novello *&* Co., where he was responsible for seeing works by Novello composers into print; through this role became close friend of Elgar; immortalised as 'Nimrod' in *Enigma Variations*. d.1909.

KODALY, ZOLTAN: b.1882. Hungarian pianist and composer. Educated Nagyszombat Gymnasium 1892–1900, Budapest University and Franz Liszt Academy of Music; taught theory at Franz Liszt Academy 1907–42; after the Second World War he travelled to England, the USA and USSR to conduct his own works. d.1967.

KREISLER, FRITZ: b.1875. Austrian-born violinist and composer. Entered Vienna Conservatoire at age seven; abandoned early musical career for studying medicine and art and later joined Austrian army; resumed music career in 1899; London debut 1901 and thereafter in the forefront of international soloists; in 1910 gave the first performance of Elgar's *Violin Concerto* which is dedicated to him. d.1972.

LEE WILLIAMS, CHARLES: b.1853. English organist and composer. Assistant organist Winchester Cathedral, 1865–70; organist Llandaff Cathedral, 1876–82; Gloucester Cathedral, 1882–97. d.1935.

LLOYD, CHARLES (HARFORD): b.1849. English organist and composer. Studied University of Oxford; organist Gloucester Cathedral 1876–82, Christ Church Cathedral, Oxford 1882–92; professor of organ and composition Royal College of Music 1887–92; musical director Eton College 1892–1914; organist Chapel Royal 1914–19. d.1919.

LLOYD, EDWARD: b.1845. English tenor. Chorister Westminster Abbey to 1860; gentleman of the Chapel Royal 1869–71; had great success at Gloucester Festival, 1871 in Bach's *St Matthew Passion*, leading to outstanding career in oratorios and cantatas; the first to sing the role of Gerontius in Elgar's *The Dream of Gerontius* in 1900, the year of his retirement. d.1927.

LLOYD, RICHARD HEY: b.1933. English organist and composer. Studied Lichfield Cathedral School and Cambridge University; sub-organist Salisbury Cathedral 1957–66; organist Hereford Cathedral 1966–74, Durham Cathedral 1974–85; deputy headmaster Salisbury Cathedral School 1985–88. d.2021.

MACFARREN, SIR GEORGE: b.1813. English composer and teacher. Studied Royal Academy of Music, later professor Royal Academy of Music 1837–87; conducted at Covent Garden from 1845; professor of music Cambridge University 1875; principal Royal Academy of Music 1875–87; blind by 1860. d.1887.

MACKENZIE, SIR ALEXANDER: b.1847. Scottish composer, violinist, conductor and teacher. Studied Sondershausen Conservatoire 1857–62, Royal Academy of Music 1862–65; principal Royal Academy of Music 1888–1924; conductor Philharmonic Society 1892–99; knighted 1895. d.1935.

MACONCHY, DAME ELIZABETH: b.1907. English composer of Irish parentage. Studied at Royal College of Music with Charles Wood and Vaughan Williams, and Prague; won Cobbett Medal for chamber music 1960. d.1994.

MANNING, JANE: b.1938. English soprano. Studied Royal Academy of Music and Switzerland; debut London 1964; visiting professor at Royal College of Music; specialist in contemporary classical music and several composers wrote works for her. d.2021.

MANNS, SIR AUGUST: b.1825. German born conductor (naturalised English). Bandmaster Konisberg and Cologne 1851–54; went to London 1854 as assistant conductor of Crystal Palace band; became conductor and augmented band to symphony orchestra 1855; between 1855 and 1901, when orchestra disbanded, Mann's concerts were the most enterprising in England; knighted 1903. d.1907.

MATHIAS, WILLIAM: b.1934. Welsh composer and pianist. Studied University College of Wales, Aberystwyth and Royal Academy of Music; lecturer in music University College of North Wales, Bangor 1959–68; senior lecturer Edinburgh University 1968–70; professor of music University College of North Wales 1970–88. d.1992.

MAXWELL DAVIES, SIR PETER: b.1934. English composer, conductor and teacher. Studied Manchester University, Royal Manchester College of Music and in Rome; musical director Cirencester Grammar School 1959–62; studied Princeton University 1962–64; co-founder chamber ensemble Fires of London 1970, for which he composed many works; from 1970 lived intermittently in Orkney; founded St Magnus Festival 1977; artistic director to Dartington International Summer School 1979–84; associate composer/ conductor BBC Philharmonic Orchestra 1992–2002; knighted 1981; Master of the Queen's Music 2004. d.2016

NEEL, (LOUIS) BOYD: b.1905. English conductor. Qualified as naval officer and medical doctor but turned to music, founding the Boyd Neel String Orchestra 1933, which became the Philomusica of London in 1957; conducted Robert Mayer Children's Concerts 1946–52; dean of Toronto Royal Conservatoire 1953–70. d.1981.

NICHOLLS, AGNES: b.1877. English soprano. Studied Royal College of Music 1894–97; opera debut London 1895; Covent Garden 1901–24; successful career in oratorio, singing in first performances of Elgar's works; married to conductor Sir Hamilton Harty. d.1959.

PARKER, HORATIO: b.1863. American composer, organist and teacher. Studied Munich Conservatoire 1881–84; held organist posts in New York; taught at National Conservatoire when Dvořák was director; organist Trinity Church, Boston 1893; professor of music Yale University 1894–1919; taught Charles Ives. d.1919.

PARRY, SIR HUBERT: b.1848. English composer, teacher and writer. Studied University of Oxford; entered business 1871 but gave it up three years later for music; joined staff Royal College of Music in 1883, becoming director 1894 until his death; professor of music University of Oxford, 1900–08; his biggest influence was through his educational work, but he was also in the forefront of British composers at a time when Brahms and Bach were the favoured models. d.1918.

PARTINGTON, ADRIAN: b.1958. English conductor, chorus master, organist and pianist. Studied Royal College of Music under Herbert Howells; organ scholar St George's Chapel, Windsor and King's College, Cambridge; assistant organist Worcester Cathedral 1981–91; associate chorus master of the City of Birmingham Symphony Orchestra chorus and conductor of the City of Birmingham Symphony Youth Chorus to 2000; director of the BBC National Orchestra and Chorus of Wales from 1999; director of Music, Gloucester Cathedral since 2008.

PIERSON, HENRY HUGO: b.1815. English/ German composer and teacher of English origin. Studied Cambridge University and in Germany; professor of music Edinburgh University 1844 for few months, then returned to Germany. d.1873.

RADFORD, ROBERT: b.1874. English bass. Studied Royal Academy of Music; opera debut Covent Garden 1904; member of Beecham and British National Opera companies; equally successful in oratorio; taught at Royal Academy of Music 1928. d.1933.

REED, WILLIAM HENRY (BILLY): b.1875. English violinist, teacher, minor composer, conductor and biographer of Sir Edward Elgar. Studied Royal Academy of Music; founding member of the London Symphony Orchestra in 1904, and its leader 1912–35; subsequently became the orchestra's chairman; also taught at Royal College of Music throughout his career; in 1936 wrote biography of Elgar, *Elgar as I knew him*. d.1942.

REEVES, SIMS (JOHN): b.1818. English tenor. Taught by father; debut 1838 then studied in Paris and Milan, singing at La Scala 1846; first sang in oratorio 1848 and thereafter appeared more often on concert platform than in opera. d.1900.

ROBINSON, CHRISTOPHER: b.1936. English conductor and organist. Organ scholar Christ Church Cathedral, Oxford; organist Worcester Cathedral 1963–74, St George's Chapel, Windsor 1974–91; organist and director of music St John's College, Cambridge 1992–2003; conductor City of Birmingham Choir 1964–2002; conductor Oxford Bach Choir 1976–97.

RUBBRA, EDMUND: b.1901. English composer and pianist. Studied at University of Reading 1920–21, Royal College of Music 1921–25, both with Holst as a tutor; lecturer University of Oxford 1947–68; professor of composition Guildhall School of Music 1961–86. d.1986.

SAINTON-DOLBY, CHARLOTTE: b.1821. English contralto. Studied Royal Academy of Music; London debut 1842; sang at Leipzig Gewandhaus Concerts 1845–46; Mendelssohn composed contralto part in *Elijah* for her; married violinist Prosper Sainton 1860; opened singing school in London 1872. d.1885.

SANDERS, JOHN: b.1933. English organist and conductor. Studied Royal College of Music and Cambridge University; assistant organist Gloucester Cathedral 1958–63; organist Chester Cathedral 1963–67; organist Gloucester Cathedral 1967–94; director of music Cheltenham Ladies College 1968–97. d.2003.

SANTLEY, SIR CHARLES: b.1834. English baritone and composer. Studied Milan and London; opera debut Pavia 1857; London concert debut 1857; sang at Scala Milan 1865–66; sang in first London Wagner opera production (*Der fliegende Hollander*) 1870; notable singer of oratorios, especially *Elijah*; knighted 1907; Covent Garden farewell 1911. d.1922.

SINCLAIR, GEORGE ROBERTSON: b.1863. English organist and conductor. Studied Royal Irish Academy of Music; assistant organist Gloucester Cathedral 1879; organist Truro Cathedral 1880–89, Hereford Cathedral 1889–1917; friend and champion of Elgar, who included him as the 11th (GRS) of *Enigma Variations*. d.1917.

SMITH, ALICE MARY (married name Alice Mary Meadows White): b.1839. English composer. Educated privately by Sterndale Bennett and George Macfarren. Elected Female Professional Associate of the Royal Philharmonic Society, 1867. Elected honorary member of the Royal Academy of Music, 1884. d.1884.

SMITH, GEORGE TOWNSEND: b.1813. English organist and conductor. Chorister St George's Chapel, Windsor; pupil of S.S. Wesley; organist of the Old Parish Church, Eastbourne; organist of Hereford Cathedral 1843–77. d.1877.

SMYTH, DAME ETHEL: b.1858. English composer and conductor. Studied Leipzig Conservatoire and Berlin; first became known through her *Mass in D*, first performed London 1893; first three operas were produced in Germany; active in militant campaign for women's suffrage and was jailed in 1911. d.1944.

STAINER, SIR JOHN: b.1840. English composer, organist, teacher and scholar. Chorister St Paul's Cathedral 1849–54; studied University of Oxford; organist St Paul's Cathedral 1872–88; professor and later principal National Training School of Music; professor of music University of Oxford from 1889. d.1901.

STANFORD, SIR CHARLES VILLIERS: b.1852. Irish composer, conductor, organist and teacher. Studied Cambridge University 1870; organist Trinity College, Cambridge 1873–92; studied in Leipzig and Berlin 1874–76; conductor Cambridge University Musical Society from 1873; professor of composition Royal College of Music 1883–1924; professor of music Cambridge University 1887–1924; conductor Bach Choir 1885–1902. d.1924.

SUDDABY, ELSIE: b.1898. English soprano. Trained as pianist but turned to singing, earning big reputation in oratorio; one of the original soloists in Vaughan Williams' *Serenade to Music*. d.1980.

SUMSION, HERBERT WHITTON (JOHN): b.1899. English organist, conductor and composer. Pupil of Brewer at Gloucester Cathedral and his assistant organist 1915–17 and 1919–22; organist Christ Church, Lancaster Gate 1922–26; director of music Bishop's Stortford College 1924–26; teacher Morley College 1924–26; studied conducting with Adrian Boult at the Royal College of Music; Professor

Curtis Institute, Philadelphia 1926–28; organist Gloucester Cathedral 1928–67; director of music Cheltenham Ladies College 1935–68. d.1995.

THURSTON, FREDERICK: b.1901. English clarinettist. Studied Royal Academy of Music; principal clarinettist BBC Symphony Orchestra 1930–46; professor of clarinet Royal College of Music 1930–53; several English composers (e.g. Bliss, Howells and Bax) composed works for him. d.1953.

TIETJENS, THERESA: b.1831. German soprano. Studied Hamburg and Vienna; opera debut Altona 1849; Frankfurt Opera 1850–56; Vienna 1856–59; London debut 1858, thereafter settling in England; one of the great opera and oratorio singers of her day, creating several Verdi roles for London. d.1877.

TUBB, CARRIE: b.1876. English soprano. Studied Guildhall School of Music. Mainly known for oratorio work but also sang opera at Covent Garden and later with the Beecham company; taught at Guildhall School of Music from 1930. d.1976.

VAUGHAN WILLIAMS, RALPH: b.1872. English composer, conductor and organist. Studied at Cambridge University and Royal College of Music, and later with Bruch and Ravel; began collecting English folk songs 1902; musical editor *English Hymnal* 1906; professor of composition Royal College of Music 1919–39; one of the leaders with Holst and others of the twentieth-century revival of English music in the wake of Elgar. d.1958.

WESLEY, SAMUEL: b.1766. English composer and organist. Child prodigy, composed part of an oratorio at age eight and published harpsichord tutor at 11; one of the earliest Bach enthusiasts and played a major role in the Bach revival; regarded as the greatest organist of his day. d.1837.

WESLEY, SAMUEL SEBASTIAN: b.1810. English composer, organist and conductor. Son of Samuel Wesley; chorister Chapel Royal; organist Hereford Cathedral 1832–35, Exeter Cathedral 1835–41, Leeds Parish Church 1842–49, Winchester Cathedral 1849–65 and Gloucester Cathedral 1865–76; professor of organ Royal Academy of Music from 1850; tireless advocate for the improvement of standards of Anglican church music. d.1876.

WILLCOCKS, SIR DAVID: b.1919. English conductor, organist, composer and teacher. Chorister Westminster Abbey 1929–34; studied Royal College of Music and Cambridge; organist Salisbury Cathedral 1947–50, Worcester Cathedral 1950–57; conductor City of Birmingham Choir 1950–57; conductor Bradford Festival Choral Society 1955–74; director of music King's College, Cambridge 1957–73; musical director Bach Choir 1960–88; director Royal College of Music 1974–84; knighted 1977. d.2015.

WOOD, CHARLES: b.1866. Irish composer and teacher. Composition pupil of Stanford at Royal College of Music, then taught harmony at same college from 1888; lecturer in harmony and counterpoint Cambridge University 1897–1924 and professor of music from 1924. d.1926.

WOOD, SIR HENRY: b.1869. English conductor and organist. Best known for conducting London's annual series of Promenade Concerts, known as 'the Proms' for nearly half a century – after his death, the concerts were officially renamed in his honour as the Henry Wood Promenade Concerts; studied Royal Academy of Music; started conducting career with small operatic touring company and then later the larger Carl Rosa Company; from mid-1890s to his death he focussed on concert conducting; initially engaged to conduct a series of promenade concerts at the Queen's Hall, offering a mixture of classical and popular music at low prices. The series was successful, and Wood conducted annual promenade series until his death in 1944. In addition to the Proms, Wood conducted concerts and festivals throughout the country and he also trained the student orchestra at the Royal Academy of Music. d.1944.

bibliography

Alldritt, Keith, *Vaughan Williams. Composer, Radical, Patriot – a Biography*, Robert Hale (2015)

Allen, Kevin, *Hugh Blair. Worcester's Forgotten Organist*, CPI Group (2019)

Atkins, Wulstan, *The Elgar Atkins Friendship*, David & Charles (1984)

Bennett, Joseph, *Forty Years of Music 1865–1905*, Methuen (1908)

Boden, Anthony & Hedley, Paul, *The Three Choirs Festival: A History*, Boydell Press (2017)

Brewer, A. Herbert, *Memories of Choirs and Cloisters*, Stainer & Bell (2015)

Burge, Kenneth, *Renaissance Years: A Three Choirs Perspective*, Three Choirs Festival (Programme article 2005)

Cobbett, William, *Rural Rides*, Penguin (1967, first published 1830)

Dibble, Jeremy, *C. Hubert Parry: His Life and Music*, Clarendon Press (1992)

Drummond, Pippa, *The Provincial Music Festival in England, 1784–1914*, Routledge (2016)

Fuller, Sophie, *Women Composers during the British Musical Renaissance 1880–1918*, King's College London PhD thesis (1998)

Gibbs, Alan, *Holst Among Friends*, Thames Publishing (2000)

Graham-Jones, Ian (ed.) *Ode to the Passions by Alice Mary Smith*, A-R Editions (2019)

Heighes, Simon John, *The Life and Works of William and Philip Hayes 1708–1777 and 1738–1797*, St Anne's College Oxford PhD thesis (1990)

Herbert, N.M. (ed.), *The Victoria History of the County of Gloucester. Volume IV The City of Gloucester*, Oxford University Press (1988)

Holst, Imogen, *Gustav Holst a Biography*, Oxford University Press (1988)

Horton, Peter, *Samuel Sebastian Wesley. A Life*, Oxford University Press (2004)

Hughes, Meirion & Stradling, Robert, *The English Musical Renaissance 1840–1940. Constructing a National Music*, Manchester University Press (2001)

Hunt, Donald, *Elgar and The Three Choirs Festival*, Osborne Heritage (1999)

Jones, Anthea, *Cheltenham, A New History*, Carnegie Publishing (2010)

Kennedy, Michael, *Portrait of Elgar*, Oxford University Press (1982)

Lysons, Revd Daniel, Amott, John, Lee Williams, Charles, Godwin Chance, H., *Origin and Progess of the Meeting of the Three Choirs* (the *Annals*), Chance & Bland (1895)

McCulloch, Matthew, 'A History and Analysis of Gerald Finzi's Dies Natalis', *British Music*, 41 (2019/1), 40–57

McVeagh, Diana, *Gerald Finzi. His Life and Music*, The Boydell Press (2005)

Moore, Jerrold Northrop, *Edward Elgar. A Creative Life*, Oxford University Press (1984)

Palmer, Christopher, *Herbert Howells. A Centenary Celebration*, Thames Publishing (1992)

Saylor, Eric, *Vaughan Williams*, Oxford University Press (2022)

Shaw, Watkins, *The Three Choirs Festival. The Official History of the Meetings of the Three Choirs of Gloucester, Hereford and Worcester,* c.*1713–1953*, Ebenezer Baylis & Son (1954)

Short, Michael, *Gustav Holst. The Man and his Music*, Circaidy Gregory Press (2014)

Spicer, Paul, *Herbert Howells*, Seren (1998)

Spicer, Paul, *Sir Arthur Bliss. Standing Out from the Crowd*, Hale (2023)

Still, Barry (ed.), *Two hundred and Fifty Years of the Three Choirs Festival*, Three Choirs Festival Association (1977)

Temperley, Nicholas (ed.), *The Athlone History of Music in Britain. Volume 5. The Romantic Age 1800–1914*, Athlone (1981)

index (main entries in **bold**; illustrations in ***bold italic***)

Albani, Dame Emma 56–7, 137

Alexandra Palace 42

All Hallows Church, Barking 98

Allen, Sir Hugh 37, 104, 139

Annals of the Three Choirs 5, 14, 21, 32, 46, 56–7, 74–9, 88, 90, 101–2, 106

Atkins, Sir Ivor 59, 66, **69**, 71, 74, **80**, 83, ***132***

Austin, Frederic 74

Bach, Johann Sebastian vi, 32, 53, 57, 61, 71, 75, 91, 97–8, 105–6, 115, 129, 137–8, 146, 148, 151

Bach Choir, London 106, 137, 141, 150, 152

Bach Choir, Oxford 143, 149

Baldwin, Stanley 66

Bantock, Granville 37, **68**, 71, 74–5, ***76***, 77, 137

Barking, All Hallows Church *see All Hallows Church, Barking*

Barnby, Sir Joseph 43

Barrett, William Alexander 43

Bath 4–5, 8, 11, 51

Bax, Sir Arnold 114, 117, 138, 151

BBC 79, 93, 104, 139

BBC National Orchestra and Chorus of Wales 128, 148

BBC Philharmonic Orchestra 147

BBC Symphony Orchestra 126, 139, 151

Beamish, Sally 51

Beard, John 3, 7, 10, 138

Beethoven, Ludwig van 16, 22, 25, 32, 36, 44, 46, 53, 57–8, 75, 99, 114–5, 128, 134, 140

Bennett, Joseph 26, 56, 58

Bennett, Sir William Sterndale 29–30, 42, 47, 49, 138, 150

Bernard, Anthony 86, 138

Bingham, Judith 51

Birmingham Brass Consort 128

Birmingham Choir, City of 149, 152

Birmingham Daily Gazette 114

Birmingham Post 99, 129

Birmingham School of Music 137

Birmingham Symphony Orchestra, City of 139, 141, 148

Birmingham Triennial Musical Festival 13, 59–61, 140

Blair, Hugh 54, 57, 59–60, 106, 138

Bliss, Sir Arthur 64, 86, **86**, 90–1, 114–5, 131, 136, 139, 151

Boisragon, Conrad 17–8
Boosey & Hawkes 31, 119
Boulez, Pierre 127
Boult, Sir Adrian 94, 129, 131, 139, 150
Boyce, William 10, 139
Boyle, Frank 44, 139
Bradford Festival Choral Society 45, 49, 152
Braham, John 18
Brahms, Johannes 22, 53, 74, 91, 99, 115, 126, 148
Brent Smith, Alexander 117, 119
Brewer, Sir Herbert xi, 48, 50–1, 60, 63, **65**, 66, 71–2, 74–5, 78–9, 85–7, 90–3, 99–102, **103**, 104–5, 108, 117, 139–40, 143–4, 150
   Brewer, Charles (son) 104
   Brewer, Eileen (daughter) 92
Bridge, Sir Frederick 55, **68**
Briggs, Kerensa 51
Brighton 5
Bristol 4, 11, 38, 47
   Cathedral 10, 139
British Broadcasting Company/ Corporation see BBC
Britten, Benjamin 83, 131, 141

Cambridge 42, 47, 138, 143–4, 146, 148–52
   Fitzwilliam Music Society 42
   King's College see King's College, Cambridge
Caradori-Allan, Maria 17–8, **19**, 140
Cardiff 57
Carrodus, John (Tiplady) 45, 140

Cheltenham 7, 18, 105–6, 116, 140, 144, 149, 151
   Music Festival 47–8, 131
Cherubini, Luigi 44, 141
Chosen Hill 116–7, 122, **122**
City of Birmingham Symphony Orchestra see Birmingham Symphony Orchestra
Clack, Richard 10
Clegg, Edith 74
Clinch, Jonathan 94
Coates, John 74, 88, 140
Cobbett, William 17
Colborne, Langdon 43–6
Coleridge-Taylor, Samuel 60, **68**
Cook, (Alfred) Melville 131, 140
Cooke, Benjamin 44
Cramer, Francois 18–9
Croft, William 9, 141
Crossley, Ada 74, 141
Crystal Palace 31, 59, 143, 147
Cusins, Sir William 49

Daily Chronicle, The 100
Daily Mail 89
Daily News 99–101, 115
Daily Telegraph, The 58, 89, 100
Dallapiccola, Luigi 128–9, 141
Davidson, Malcolm 117
Davies, Meredith 122, 131, **132**, 141
Davies, (Henry) Walford 61, **68**, 71, 99–100, 102, 141
Decca Records 80
Delius, Frederick 105
Dommett, Kenneth 129

Done, William 26, 54

Doolittle, Emily 51

D'Oyly Carte Opera Company 44, 139–40

Dutton Vocalion 80

Dvořák, Antonín 53, 129, 148

Elgar, Edward 37, 39, 49, **52–69**, 71–2, 74–9, **78**, **81**, 85–8, 91, 94, 97–8, 102, 104, **107**, 115, 117, 129, 131, 137–41, 145–9, 151
  Alice (wife of, née Roberts) 54

Ellicott, Rosalind **40**, 41, **47–49**, 60, 142

Elvey, George 29

Eton School 27, 29–30, 35, 37, 138, 146

Faber Music Limited 98

Fenna, Marian 45

Ferguson, Howard 118, 120, 122, 142

Feshareki, Shiva 51

Festival chorus **ii**, 1, 9, 13, 15, 19, 25, 32, 36, 38, **45**, 51, 57, **60**, **65**, 71, 75, 88, 99–101, 106, **111**, 121, **123**, **124**, 125, 128–9, **133**, 134–6

Festival of the Sons of the Clergy 10

Festival orchestra 1, 3, 10, 13–5, 18–20, 25–6, 29, 32, 36, 38, 45, 51, 54, 57, 59, 71, 74–5, 77, 79, 90, 98, 114, 121, 129, 134, 136

Finzi, Gerald 94, **112–123**, 131, 142
  Joy (wife of) 113, 117–8, **118**, 122

Fischer, Christian (Johann) 10, 142

Frances-Hoad, Cheryl 51

Frasi, Giulia 3, 7, 10

Galli, Signora 10

Gibbons, Orlando 99, 101, 104

Gleeson-White, Cicely 74

Gloucester 1–11, **8**, 17, 20–1, 25–7, 30–3, 37, 39, 43–4, 47–51, 57, 60–1, 63, 65, 71–5, 77–9, 83, 85–6, 90–4, 97, 101–5, 108, 110, 116–7, 121–2, 125, 131, 133, **133**, 142, 146
  9, College Green **78**, 79
  Boothall, the 1–3, **2**, 5–6
  Cathedral 9, 21, 25, 29, **31**, 71–2, **73**, 75, 85, 87, **90**, 91–2, 97, 101, 121, **135**, 139–140, 143–6, 148–51
  Choral Society 25, 45
  Highnam Court see Highnam Court
  races 5, **6**
  Shire Hall 3, **27**, 37, 75, 78, 104

Gloucester Citizen 105

Gloucester Journal 50, 90, **103**

Gloucestershire Chronicle 35

Gloucestershire Philharmonic Society 47

Godfrey, Dan 72, 142

Goetz, Hermann 74

Goossens, Sir Eugene 63, 86, 90–1, 142

Gounod, Charles 32, 53, 58, 140

Greene, Eric 121

Greene, Harry Plunket 58, 74, 107, 142

Greene, Maurice 9

Grove, Sir George 31, 35, 37, 143

Guadagni, Gaetano 10

Gurney, Ivor 75, 77, 85, 91, 116–7, 120, 143

Hackney Choral Association 49

Hadow, Sir Henry 37

Handel, George Frideric *xii*, **1–11**, 15–6, 18, 21, 25, 29, 31, 36, 38, 71, 74, 114, 127, 129, 136, 138, 143

Handel Society Choir, London 47

Harding, Charlotte 51

Harvey, Jonathan 128–9, 143

Harwood, Basil 74–5, 77, 79, 143

Haydn, Joseph 14, 16, 18, 25, 32–3, 53, 57, 114

Hayes, William 1–4, *4*, 7–8, 10–11, 44, 143

Herbert, Maud 35

Hereford 7–22, *12*, 29, 46–7, 49, 59, *60*, 61–3, *62*, *63*, 65–6, *69*, 80, 83, 97, 104, 107, 109, 113, 116, *118*, 119, 129–31, 139–40

  Cathedral 3, 11, *12*, 13, 20, *21*, 25, 43, 45, *60*, *62*, *65*, *69*, *111*, 113, *118*, 119, 140–1, 144, 146, 149–51

  Choral Society 25, 45

  Shire Hall 41, 44–5, *45*

Hereford Journal 16, 22

Hereford Music Room 9

Hereford Times 14–5, 17, 22, 129

Hess, Dame Myra 120, 144

Highnam Court 28–9, *28*

Higley, William 74

Holst, Gustav 39, 63, **96–111**, 115, 121, 126, 131, 139, 144, 149, 151

  Holst, Imogen (daughter of) 98, 106, 108

  Von Holst, Adolph (father of) 106

Holywell Music Room 4, 144

Howard, Dani 51

Howells, Herbert 63, 75, 77, **84–95**, 105, 110, 116–7, 120–2, 131, 144, 148, 151

  Howells, Dorothy (wife of) 117

  Howells, Michael (son of) 93–5

Hueffer, Francis 46

Hull, Sir Percy 63, 66, *69*, *111*, 119, 144

Hummel, Johann Nepomuk 125–6

Hunt, Donald 131, 145

Ireland, John 86, 145

Jaeger, August 145

Janáček, Leos 129, 134

Jones, Mildred 74

King, Frederick 44

King's College, Cambridge 138, 144, 148, 152

King's College, London 47

Knyvett, William 17–8

Kodaly, Zoltan 115, 145

Kreisler, Fritz 74–5, 79, *81*, 145

Lee Williams, Charles 57, 74, 78–9, 86, 145

Leeds 57, 140, 145, 151

Leeds chorus 57, 106

Leeds Festival 57, 60, 106

Leppard, Raymond 131

Lett, Phyllis 74

Lloyd, Charles (Harford) 43, 57–8, 75, 146

Lloyd, Edward 57–8, 146

Lloyd, Richard Hey 129, 131, 146
Loder, John 19
London 1, 4–5, 9–10, 18, *19*, 20, 25–6,
   31, 33, 38, 41–2, 44, 47, 49, 54–5,
   58–9, 65, 79, *81*, 105, 117, 138, 140–3,
   145–7, 149–51
   Alexandra Palace *see Alexandra
      Palace*
   Crystal Palace *see Crystal Palace*
   Hackney Choral Association *see
      Hackney Choral Association*
   Handel Society *see Handel Society*
   King's College *see King's College,
      London*
   Morley College *see Morley College,
      London*
   National Gallery *see National
      Gallery, London*
   Philharmonic Society *see
      Philharmonic Society, Royal*
   Queen's Hall *see Queen's Hall,
      London*
   Royal College of Music *see Royal
      College of Music*
   St James Hall *see St James Hall*
   St Paul's Cathedral, London
      see St Paul's Cathedral, London
   St Paul's Girls' School
      see St Paul's Girls' School, London
   Westminster Abbey *see Westminster
      Abbey*
   Wigmore Hall *see Wigmore Hall*
London Symphony Orchestra *65*, 74,
   88, 114–5, 148
Lydney 91

Macfarren, Sir George 42, 146, 150
Mackenzie, Sir Alexander 53, **68**, 146
Maconchy, Dame Elizabeth 51, 128, 146
Manchester Guardian 58, 67, 69, 99
Mann, William 130
Manning, Jane 128, 146
Manns, Sir August 59, 147
Mathias, William 128, 147
Maxwell Davies, Peter 129, 147
McCune, Sally Lamb 51
McVeagh, Diana 116, 121
Mendelssohn, Felix 16, 25, 29–33,
   35–6, 38, 53, 57, 66, 75, 88, 149
Merewether, Dr John 20
Miller, John 125–6, **126**
Mori, Nicholas 19
Morley College, London 98, 144, 150
Morning Post, The 50, 89
Mozart, Wolfgang Amadeus 16, 21–2,
   53, 57, 115
Musical Opinion 101
Musical Times, The 48, 57–8, 76–7,
   79, 89, 101–2, 104, 106, 114

National Gallery, London 120, 144
National Youth Orchestra 125–7, **126**,
   143
Neel, (Louis) Boyd 80, 147
Neukomm, Sigismund 21
Newbury String Players 121
Nicholls, Agnes 74, 147
Norfolk and Norwich Festival 13
Northern Sinfonia 126
Novello & Co. 39, 43, 48, 55, 98, 119, 145
Novello, Ivor 85

organ 15–6, 28, 30, 32, 36, 74, 77–8, 83, 87, 92, 94, 107, 121, 138–40, 143, 146, 148–9, 151

Oxford 1–2, 4, 11, 27, 38, 44, 49, 123, 130, 137, 139, 143–4, 146, 148–50

Oxford Journal 5–6

Oxford University Press 119

Palmer, Christopher 94

Parker, Horatio 61, 148

Parry, Sir Hubert 22, **24–39**, 53, 57, 59, 63, 68, 71, 74–5, 78–9, 91–2, 99, 104, 115, 117, 121, 142, 148

  Thomas Gambier (father of) 27–8

Partington, Adrian 128, 133, **135**, 148

Philharmonia Orchestra 127

Philharmonic Italian Opera 20

Philharmonic Orchestra, Royal 128–9

Philharmonic Society, Royal 16, 42, 49, 138, 146, 150

Philip Jones Brass Ensemble 127

Phillips, Henry 17, 22

Pickup, Muriel 74

Pierson, Henry Hugo 29, 35, 148

Plunket Greene, Harry 58, 74, 107, 142

Promenade Concerts 92–3, 139, 152

Prout, Dr Ebenezer 46, 49, **68**

Queen's Hall, London 92, 142, 152

Radford, Robert 74, 148

Reed, William Henry (Billy) 51, 66, 74, **78**, 79, 86, 88, 119, 148

Reeves, Sims (John) 31, **32**, 149

Reynish, Timothy 126

Rignold, Hugo 131

Robinson, Christopher 125, 128–9, 131, 149

Rossini, Gioachino 53, 129

Royal Academy of Music 44, 47, 137–8, 142, 144, 146–52

Royal College of Music 37, 44, 80, 85, 93–4, 105, 107, 119, 137, 139, 141–52

Royal Northern College of Music 127

Royal Philharmonic Orchestra *see Philharmonic Orchestra*

Royal Philharmonic Society *see Philharmonic Society*

Royal Societies Club 86

Rubbra, Edmund 122, 149

Sainton-Dolby, Charlotte 31, 149

Salisbury 8, 11

  Cathedral 92, 144, 146, 152

Sanders, John 131, 149

Santley, Sir Charles 31, 149

Savage, William 10

Schellhorn, Matthew 94

Schubert, Franz 31, 126, 129

Schumann, Robert 22, 92, 129, 138

Schuster, Frank 61

Schwarz, Rudolph 126–7

Scott, Cyril **68**

Scott, Sir Walter 55

Shaw, George Bernard 66

Sheffield Daily Telegraph 99

Short, Michael 100

Sibelius, Jean 78, 104

Simpson, Amy 74

Sinclair, George Robertson *45*, 59, 63, 71, 107, 144, 149

Skillicorne, Henry 7

Smith, Alice Mary **41–9**, 150

Smith, George Townsend 26, 150

Smyth, Dame Ethel **49–51**, *68*, 97–8, 102, *103*, 105, 150

Sparkhall, Olivia 51

Spicer, Paul 85–6, 90

Spohr, Louis 14, 16, 21–2, 29, 31, 33, 36, 53, 57

St James Hall 49

St Paul's Cathedral, London 9, 139, 144, 150

St Paul's Girls' School, London 98, 144

Stainer, Sir John 37, 53, 150

Stanford, Sir Charles Villiers 37, 68, 75, 92, 142, 150, 152

stewards 4–7, *7*, 10, 14, 21, 27, 32, 102, 104, 135

Stockhausen, Margarethe 18

Strauss, Richard 75

Stravinsky, Igor 129, 131, 134

Stuart-Wortley, Alice 61

Suddaby, Elsie 120, 150

Sullivan, Arthur 35–6, 53, 74

Sumsion, Herbert Whitton (John) 51, 66, *69*, *80*, 92–4, 114–8, *118*, 120–1, 131, *132*, 140, 145, 150

Alice (wife of) *80*, 117–8, *118*, 122

Tabakova, Dobrinka 51

Tann, Hilary 51

Tertis, Lionel 64

Thurston, Frederick 114–5, 151

Tietjens, Theresa 31, 33, 151

Times, The 46, 72, 88, 99, 130

Traherne, Thomas 119

Tubb, Carrie 88, 151

Vaughan, Henry 17, 97, 100

Vaughan Williams, Dr Ralph 64, 66, **70–83**, 87, 92, 94, 97–9, 101, 104, 106, 109, *109*, 113–5, 117, 120–2, *123*, 131, 139, 142, 146, 150–1

Adeline (1st wife of, d.1951) 121

Ursula (2nd wife of, née Lock, formerly Wood) 72, *82*, 113–4, 122–4

Verdi, Giuseppe 53, 71, 75, 91, 115, 151

Vesuvius Ensemble 128

Victoria, Queen 43

Wagner, Richard 38, 48, 53, 57, 59, 71, 91, 116, 149

Walton, William 64, 125, 131

Watkin-Mills, Robert 58, 107

Weber, Carl Maria von 31, 57

Webb, Frank 59

Wesley, Samuel 15, 25, 32–3, 115, 151

Wesley, Samuel Sebastian 11, 14–5, **20–3**, 25–7, 29–33, 36–7, 47, 74, 142, 150–1

Western Daily Press 115

Westminster Abbey 9, 44, 55, 140, 146, 152

Whitsuntide singers 98

Whittaker, William G. 109

Wigmore Hall 120

Willcocks, Sir David 122, 131, *132*, 152

Williams, Anna 44, 58

Williamson, Malcolm 129

Wilson, Hilda 45, 56, 107

Wood, Charles 92, 101, 146, 152

Wood, Sir Henry 72, 92, 152

Wood, Ursula *see Vaughan Williams*

Worcester 5, 8–10, 17, 21, 51, 53–5,
  58–61, 63–6, 68, 80, *80*, *82*, 83,
  105–6, *123*, 125, 128–9, 131–4, *132*,
  136, 145

  Cathedral 1, 4, 13, *23*, *34*, 67, 94,
    117, *124*, 125, 137–8, 141, 143, 145,
    148–9, 152

  Festival Choral Society 25, 45

  Guildhall 9

  Public Hall 53, 57, 59–60

Worcester Weekly Journal 5

Worthington, Julia 61